# Perspectives on the Nature of Christ in the Ethiopian Orthodox Church

# A Case Study in Contextualized Theology

By Stephen J. Strauss

William Carey International University Press

Pasadena, CA

Stephen J. Strauss

*Perspectives on the Nature of Christ in the Ethopian Orthodox Church: A Case Study in Contextualized Theology*

William Carey International University Press

1539 E. Howard Street, Pasadena, California 91104

E-mail: wciupress@wciu.edu

www.wciupress.org

Copyright © 2014 by Stephen J. Strauss

Except as provided by the Copyright Act, no part of this publication may be reproduced, stored in a retrieval system or transmitted in any form or by any means without the prior written permission of the publisher.

All rights reserved

ISBN: 9780865850484

Library of Congress Control Number: 2014930314

# Editor's Preface

In order to encourage and make known Evangelical missiological scholarship the Evangelical Missiological Society (EMS) launched a dissertation series in 2010. In collaboration with William Carey International University Press, the Society is publishing up to four dissertations per year that its reviewers have judged as scholarly, relevant, and timely for advancing the global cause of Christ. We pray you will find this dissertation informative and stimulating.

Thomas J. Sappington, Editor

EMS Dissertation Series

# EMS DISSERTATION SERIES

Series Editor: Tom Sappington

## Reviewers for 2012

Mike Barnett, Columbia International University
Bruce Carlton, Oklahoma Baptist University
John Chesworth, University of Oxford
Howard Culbertson, Southern Nazarene University
Cheryl Doss, Andrews University
Robert Gallagher, Wheaton College
Anthony Greenham, Southeastern Baptist Theological Seminary
Charles Kraft, Fuller Theological Seminary
Bob Lenz, The Evangelical Alliance Mission
Alan McMahan, Biola University
Garry Morgan, Northwestern College
Harold Netland, Trinity Evangelical Divinity School
Kyeong-Sook Park, Moody Bible Institute
David Sills, Southern Baptist Theological Seminary
Fred Smith, Toccoa Falls College
Beth Snodderly, William Carey International University
Tom Steffen, Biola University
Steve Strauss, Dallas Theological Seminary

PERSPECTIVES ON THE NATURE OF CHRIST IN THE
ETHIOPIAN ORTHODOX CHURCH: A CASE STUDY
IN CONTEXTUALIZED THEOLOGY


by

Stephen J. Strauss

B.A., Bryan College, 1976
Th.M., Dallas Theological Seminary, 1980


A DISSERTATION

Submitted to the Faculty
in partial fulfillment of the requirements
for the degree of
DOCTOR OF PHILOSOPHY
at Trinity International University


Deerfield, Illinois
December 1997

Accepted:

_____
Dissertation Director

_____
Second Reader

_____
Ex Officio

ABSTRACT

The Ethiopian Orthodox Church (EOC) is non-Chalcedonian, believing that Christ's human and divine natures combined into one nature which is both human and divine. Do Western and Ethiopian Orthodox Christians have the same Christology, but express it differently? If not, how are they different? How should evangelicals in Ethiopia express their understanding of Christ's deity and humanity so that they are clear, unoffensive, and biblical?

To answer these questions one must understand historical, formal, linguistic, and popular perspectives on the nature of Christ in the EOC. Historically, non-Chalcedonian Christology has increasingly been identified with authentically Ethiopian Christianity. Formally, the EOC affirms the full deity and humanity of Christ in one nature, but stresses the unity of his person. Linguistically, it is difficult to express the idea of "two natures in one person" in Amharic or Ge'ez.

An ethnographic study of one Addis Ababa neighborhood was conducted to begin to understand popular perspectives on the nature of Christ in the EOC. Subjects in this neighborhood agreed that Christ was both God and man, but many seemed to feel his humanity was different from that of other people. Most subjects felt that Christ had only one nature, that following his ascension to heaven he was only God, and that he is not now an intercessor-mediator to God.

Biblically-centered contextual theology is the best framework for evaluating these perspectives. Cultural context affects the awareness interpreters have of aspects of the text, shapes theological forms, and raises questions for theologizing. However, priority must be given to the biblical paradigm in theologizing, theological understanding may be shared across time and cultures, and the relationship of form and meaning in theologizing must be viewed on a continuum. The findings support this perspective on contextual theology.

The findings suggest that there are some substantive differences between Chalcedonian and Ethiopian Orthodox perspectives on the nature of Christ. In speaking of Christ, evangelicals in Ethiopia should avoid referring to "two natures" while affirming his full deity and, especially, his full humanity. They should develop a fresh Christological creed for the Ethiopian context.

To Marcia, Cara, Mark and David, God's greatest gifts to me and his good instruments for helping me come to know Jesus Christ

TABLE OF CONTENTS

ABSTRACT . . . . . . . . . . . . . . . . . . . . . . . . . . iii

ACKNOWLEDGMENTS. . . . . . . . . . . . . . . . . . . . . . . xi

Chapter

1. THE RESEARCH PROBLEM . . . . . . . . . . . . . . . . . 1

    Research Concern. . . . . . . . . . . . . . . . . . 1

    Research Question . . . . . . . . . . . . . . . . . 3

    Assumptions . . . . . . . . . . . . . . . . . . . . 5

    Delimitations . . . . . . . . . . . . . . . . . . . 6

        Members of the Ethiopian Orthodox Church . . . 6

        The Alert Hospital/Gebre Kristos Neighborhood of Addis Ababa. . . . . . . . . . . . . . . . 7

    Limitations . . . . . . . . . . . . . . . . . . . . 9

    Definitions . . . . . . . . . . . . . . . . . . . . 10

        Evangelical. . . . . . . . . . . . . . . . . . 10

        "Nature" and "Person" of Christ. . . . . . . . 12

        Priest, Monk, *Debtara*, Deacon. . . . . . . . . 12

        "Monophysite" and "Non-Chalcedonian" . . . . . 14

    Overview of the Procedure . . . . . . . . . . . . . 15

2. LITERATURE REVIEW. . . . . . . . . . . . . . . . . . . 18

    History, Theology and Theological Terms of the Ethiopian Orthodox Church. . . . . . . . . . . . 18

    History of the Nature of Christ in the Ethiopian Orthodox Church . . . . . . . . . . 19

    Formal Theology of the Nature of Christ in the Ethiopian Orthodox Church . . . . . . . 24

    Theological Framework for Evaluation. . . . . . . . 28

        Theology in Context. . . . . . . . . . . . . . 29

      A Christological Framework . . . . . . . . . . . 39

      Research Theory and Method. . . . . . . . . . . . 40

        Historiographic Method . . . . . . . . . . . 40

        Anthropological Framework and Ethnographic
          Research Methodology. . . . . . . . . . . 42

3. THE CONTEXT: HISTORICAL, FORMAL, AND LINGUISTICS
PERSPECTIVES ON THE NATURE OF CHRIST IN THE
ETHIOPIAN ORTHODOX CHURCH. . . . . . . . . . . . . . 49

      Historical Perspectives on the Nature of Christ
        in the Ethiopian Orthodox Church . . . . . . 49

        The Establishment of Non-Chalcedonian
          Christianity in Ethiopia. . . . . . . . . 50

        Ethiopian Orthodoxy Interacts
          with the West . . . . . . . . . . . . . . 63

        Orthodoxy's Internal Debates Over the Nature
          of Christ . . . . . . . . . . . . . . . . 78

      Formal Perspectives on the Nature of Christ
        in the Ethiopian Orthodox Church. . . . . . . 85

        Official Publications of the Ethiopian
          Orthodox Church. . . . . . . . . . . . . 86

        Other Ethiopian Orthodox Writers. . . . . . . 91

      Linguistic Perspectives on the Nature of Christ
        in the Ethiopian Orthodox Church . . . . . . 93

      Conclusion. . . . . . . . . . . . . . . . . . . . 97

4. RESEARCH METHODOLOGY . . . . . . . . . . . . . . . 100

      Operational Questions . . . . . . . . . . . . . . 101

      Population. . . . . . . . . . . . . . . . . . . . 101

      Selection of Subjects . . . . . . . . . . . . . . 102

      Instrument. . . . . . . . . . . . . . . . . . . . 107

        Interview Questions. . . . . . . . . . . . . 108

        Analysis of Interview Questions. . . . . . . 109

    Conduct of Interviews and Recording
        Interview Results. . . . . . . . . . . . . 111

    Analysis of Field Notes . . . . . . . . . . . . 115

    Overview of Procedure . . . . . . . . . . . . . 116

5. FINDINGS . . . . . . . . . . . . . . . . . . . . . 118

    The "Nature" of Christ. . . . . . . . . . . . . 118

        Christ's Nature Described as
          Ethiopian Orthodoxy . . . . . . . . . . 119

        Beyond Understanding . . . . . . . . . . . . 120

        The Work of Christ: Savior,
          Example and Teacher . . . . . . . . . . 122

        Christ's Ontological Character . . . . . . . 124

        Summary. . . . . . . . . . . . . . . . . . . 127

    God, Man or God-Man When on Earth?. . . . . . . 128

        Both God and Man . . . . . . . . . . . . . . 128

        Only God . . . . . . . . . . . . . . . . . . 141

        Only Man . . . . . . . . . . . . . . . . . . 141

        Summary: The God-Man, But Less than Truly
          Man . . . . . . . . . . . . . . . . . . 142

    God or Man Now? . . . . . . . . . . . . . . . . 143

    How Many Natures? . . . . . . . . . . . . . . . 144

        Only One Nature. . . . . . . . . . . . . . . 145

        Two Natures. . . . . . . . . . . . . . . . . 151

        Summary: One Nature. . . . . . . . . . . . . 153

    Christ As Intercessor-Mediator. . . . . . . . . 154

        Christ is Not an *Amalaj*. . . . . . . . . . . 155

        Other *Amalajoch*. . . . . . . . . . . . . . . 158

        Christ Is an *Amalaj*. . . . . . . . . . . . . 164

  Summary: Christ is Not an
   Intercessor-Mediator. . . . . . . . . . . . . 165

 A Relationship With Christ. . . . . . . . . . . . . 166

  A Relationship of Prayer . . . . . . . . . . . 166

  Women: A Relationship of Love. . . . . . . . . 167

  Laymen and Clergy: A Relationship of Distance
   and Submission. . . . . . . . . . . . . . . . 167

  Clergy: A Relationship Through the
   Eucharist . . . . . . . . . . . . . . . . . . 169

  A Relationship of Faith. . . . . . . . . . . . 169

 Summary: Popular Perspectives on the Nature
  of Christ Among Ethiopian Orthodox in Alert/
  Gebre Kristos, Addis Ababa . . . . . . . . . . 170

6. FRAMEWORK FOR THEOLOGICAL AND MISSIOLOGICAL
 REFLECTION . . . . . . . . . . . . . . . . . . . . . . 172

 Theology in Context . . . . . . . . . . . . . . . . 172

  Exegesis-Centered and Context-Centered
   Models for Theologizing . . . . . . . . . . . 173

  Biblically-Centered Contextual Theologizing. . 177

 A Comparative Chalcedonian Christology. . . . . . . 206

  The Appropriateness of Erickson's
   Christology . . . . . . . . . . . . . . . . . 207

  Erickson's Christology . . . . . . . . . . . . 209

7. CONCLUSIONS. . . . . . . . . . . . . . . . . . . . . . 213

 Reflections on Research Findings. . . . . . . . . . 213

 Christological Theologizing in Ethiopia . . . . . . 216

  General Principles . . . . . . . . . . . . . . 216

  Specific Suggestions . . . . . . . . . . . . . 218

 Implications for Biblically-Centered Contextual
  Theologizing . . . . . . . . . . . . . . . . . . 225

  The Contextual Nature of Theology. . . . . . . 225

    Awareness of Aspects of the Text . . . . . . . 226
    Form and Meaning . . . . . . . . . . . . . . . 226
    Inter-cultural Theologizing. . . . . . . . . . 227
    Use of Creeds and Historical Theology. . . . . 228
    Relationship Between Reflection and Action . . 230
  Suggestions for Missionary Training . . . . . . . 231
  Suggestions for Further Study . . . . . . . . . . 232
  Conclusion. . . . . . . . . . . . . . . . . . . . 234

Appendix

  A. EOC POSITIONS ON CHRIST'S ANOINTING. . . . . . . . 235

  B. CHRISTOLOGICAL CREEDS WRITTEN BY STUDENTS OF THE
     EVANGELICAL THEOLOGICAL COLLEGE OF ADDIS ABABA . . . 236

GLOSSARY OF AMHARIC TERMS. . . . . . . . . . . . . . . 240

REFERENCE LIST . . . . . . . . . . . . . . . . . . . . 242

## ACKNOWLEDGMENTS

Special thanks to Dr. Seeyoum Gebre Sellasie, Estifanos Yohannes, Addis Gizaw, and the students of the Evangelical Theological College, who helped ensure clear communication between this *fereng* and his subjects, and to the clergy of the Gebre Kristos Church of Addis Ababa who tolerated hearing the same questions over and over again.

# CHAPTER 1
## THE RESEARCH PROBLEM

One of the distinctive characteristics of the Ethiopian Orthodox Church has been its rejection of the Chalcedonian understanding of the person of Christ. Ever since the Council of Chalcedon (A.D. 451), the Western church has described Christ as having two natures, one divine and one human, combined in one person. However the Ethiopian Orthodox Church has understood the human and divine natures of Christ to have united into one nature which is both divine and human. The Ethiopian Orthodox Church's position has often been labeled "monophysitism" by Chalcedonian theologians, though the Ethiopian church itself rejects that label (Aymro and Joachim 1970, 97). Over the centuries this issue has divided the Ethiopian Orthodox Church from the Western theological tradition of both the Roman Catholic and Protestant churches.

### Research Concern

Christology is central to Christian theology. At the very heart of what Christians believe is their understanding and description of the person of Jesus Christ. Furthermore, as in any theological description, historical and cultural context will strongly influence the way Christians shape their

Christology. Therefore, present understandings of Jesus Christ in the Ethiopian context will be strongly influenced by the historical and cultural context of the Ethiopian Orthodox Church's non-Chalcedonian understanding of the nature of Christ. In particular, Christians from an Ethiopian Orthodox background and Christians from the Western theological tradition must determine how they will respond to one another's Christologies. Do they have an identical understanding of the person of Christ? If so, why do they express it so differently? If not, what are their differences? How should Ethiopian and expatriate evangelicals living in Ethiopia "do theology" of Christ in their own particular context? Should they identify themselves as those who believe in one nature of Christ or two? How will the Orthodox understand them and respond if evangelicals emphasize belief in Christ's two natures? If evangelicals share their faith with Orthodox believers, should they emphasize that the Jesus in whom they believe has two natures? Should evangelical converts from Ethiopian Orthodoxy be taught that Jesus has two natures? How should the issue of Christ's nature(s) be raised in evangelical theological education programs?

Questions about comparative Chalcedonian and non-Chalcedonian Christologies raise larger questions about the contextual nature of theology. When different theologies emerge from different historical and cultural traditions, is it possible that they are *different* without being *disparate*? If so, how does one determine if the differences are complementary or conflicting? Can fundamentally conflicting and disparate interpretations developed by two theological communities be equally faithful to the biblical text which they have used as a source? To what extent are theological differences the product of exegesis, presumably with the possibility of a resolution, and to what extent are they the product of culture and history? What is the role of creeds and historical theology in providing a theological norm for the universal church, particularly in relation to proliferating "local theologies" (Schreiter 1985)? The differing Christologies of Chalcedon and the Ethiopian Orthodox Church raise questions which must be answered within the framework of the contextual nature of theology; answers to those questions will provide fresh perspectives in the larger discussion on the globalization and contextualization of theology.

## Research Question

Before missiological and theological questions such as these can be answered, however, there is a prior question that must be answered: how exactly do the Ethiopian Orthodox understand the nature of Christ? What do they mean when they say that Christ has one nature? The question must be approached in four ways: (1) How did the non-Chalcedonian doctrine of the nature of Christ develop in Ethiopia? (2) How do the Orthodox explain the doctrine of the one nature of Christ in their formal writings? (3) What are the implications for the words used for "nature" used in Ethiopia's national and ecclesiastical languages? (4) How do Orthodox individuals actually describe their understanding of the nature of Christ? The four questions are closely related. One would expect the formal and popular statements of the doctrine to be similar, but not identical. However, theology must be developed in the context of what people actually believe and practice, so an understanding of popular perspectives of the nature of Christ, even if they are distinct from formal teaching about his nature, is absolutely essential. Language is fundamental to both understanding and communication; both official and popular perspectives on the nature of Christ will be strongly conditioned by the field of meaning of the words for "nature."

Finally, neither the official nor the popular descriptions of the nature of Christ can be understood apart from the doctrine's historical development. Geertz (1968) provides a good example of the importance of historical background to any contemporary ethnographic analysis, especially that of religion. Therefore, before Christological theologizing in the Ethiopian context can take place, a further understanding of perspectives on the nature of Christ in the Ethiopian Orthodox Church is needed.

Ethiopia is a large country, and it would be possible to investigate perspectives on the nature of Christ among Orthodox in many parts of the country. However, in order to do adequate "thick description" (Geertz 1973) of how the Orthodox themselves actually describe Christ, research will be limited to one urban neighborhood in the country's capital city of Addis Ababa. The research question, then, is "What do members of the Ethiopian Orthodox Church in one urban community believe about the nature of Christ?"

## Assumptions

For the purpose of this thesis, it is assumed that the historical development of non-Chalcedonian Christology in the Ethiopian Orthodox Church and the church's formal understanding of the nature of Christ have been adequately studied and can be understood from available literature. Because these historical and formal perspectives on the nature of Christ are extremely significant to understanding current popular perspectives on the nature of Christ, the conclusions of this literature will be surveyed in some depth, but a fresh interpretation will not be attempted. Rather, the focus of research will be on popular perspectives on the nature of Christ in the Ethiopian Orthodox Church and on the significance of these perspectives to the task of theologizing in Ethiopia.

## Delimitations

The study has been delimited to those who identify themselves as members of the Ethiopian Orthodox Church who live in the Alert Hospital/Gebre Kristos neighborhood of Addis Ababa.

## Members of The Ethiopian Orthodox Church

The focus of the research is on perceptions of Christ in the Ethiopian Orthodox Church, therefore the research has been delimited to those who identify themselves as members of the Ethiopian Orthodox Church. Most people in Ethiopia are born into Muslim or Ethiopian Orthodox families,[1] and their usual perception is that one's religion is a matter of birth. It is understood that people are born either as Orthodox or as Muslims, and they remain as they are born for their entire lives. Ethiopians who are not Muslims or who do not otherwise identify themselves as outside the Orthodox Church or members of another religion are considered to be Ethiopian Orthodox. (Ephraim 1971, 266). In addition, in recent years, the government of Ethiopia has occasionally surveyed the country's population and asked, "What is your religion (Amharic: *Haimanot*)? This question has been asked all research subjects. Those answering simply "Christian" (an answer which, until recently, always meant a member of the Orthodox church) have been asked whether they are Orthodox Christians.

---

[1] Approximately 35% of Ethiopia's people are Muslims and 43% are Ethiopian Orthodox (Johnstone 1993, 213-14).

Only those identifying themselves are Orthodox Christians have been included as subjects. Several potential interviewees who were assumed to be Orthodox Christians identified themselves as "no longer Orthodox" and so were not included as subjects.[2]

## The Alert Hospital/Gebre Kristos Neighborhood of Addis Ababa

The study was conducted in a single neighborhood in southwestern Addis Ababa. The central landmark of this neighborhood is the All Africa Leprosy Rehabilitation and Training Centre, commonly called "Alert". The hospital was previously named Princess Zenebe Werk Hospital (named for one of the daughters of former Emperor Haile Selassie), and the neighborhood is popularly known as "Zenebe Werk." The hospital was founded in 1932 by Dr. Thomas Lambie and is now an autonomous research, training and treatment center attracting leprosy specialists from all over the world for research and further training. The hospital has also attracted many leprosy patients from throughout Ethiopia, many who have brought their families and have settled near the hospital.

---

[2]As noted in Chapter 4, three target groups were identified based on typical levels of theological education--laywomen, laymen, and clergy--and subjects were selected from all three groups. Within these three groups, an attempt was made to select subjects who were both regular and irregular in their church attendance, in order to represent a cross section of typical Ethiopian Orthodox. Analysis of the interviews took into consideration the level of church involvement as well as whether subjects were laywomen, laymen, or clergy. See Chapter 4 for a complete description of how subjects were selected and how interviews were analyzed.

Standing beside the Alert Hospital compound and in the center of the entire neighborhood is the Gebre Kristos ("Servant of Christ") Orthodox Church. Ethiopian Orthodox churches are named for one of many saints honored by the church, and Ethiopian Orthodox Christians usually make an effort to attend the church named for their favorite saint, particularly on days set aside to honor that saint. However, the central location of Gebre Kristos Church makes it the most convenient church for most Orthodox Christians in the Alert neighborhood to attend. All subjects indicated that they attended Gebre Kristos church at least occasionally, even if they also frequented another church in order to honor that church's saint. Except for one monk, all clergy interviewed were serving at the Gebre Kristos church at the time of the interview.

Alert Hospital and the Gebre Kristos church stand immediately to the east of the Jimma Road, the main road running out of Addis Ababa to the southwest. The official government designation for the Alert/Gebre Kristos neighborhood is Wereda 24, Kebelle 15 (west of the Jimma Road) and Wereda 23, Kebelle 16 (east of the Jimma Road). All subjects were residents of one of these two urban precincts at the time they were interviewed. At the time the interviews took place, the population of Wereda 24, Kebelle 15 was about 25,000 living in 2,375 homes (Bekele 1995) and the population of Wereda 23, Kebelle 16 was 30,000-40,000 living in 3500-4000 homes (Alemu 1996).[3]

The Alert/Gebre Kristos neighborhood was chosen as the focus for research for several reasons. First, the researcher had lived in the area for thirteen years when the interviews began, and so was somewhat known in the neighborhood. This greatly facilitated the willingness of subjects to grant him interviews. Second, the presence of Gebre Kristos church at the center of the neighborhood provided a common and convenient place to meet potential subjects and a comfortable reference point for subjects who could identify it as "their church." Third, the neighborhood is made up of people from many of Ethiopia's ethnic groups. Adherents of the Ethiopian Orthodox Church from many ethnic groups can be found living side by side.

## Limitations

Findings will only be directly relevant to members of the Ethiopian Orthodox Church in the Alert/Gebre Kristos neighborhood of Addis Ababa. Specifically, the findings will help evangelicals in the Alert/Gebre Kristos neighborhood to understand and respond appropriately as they "do theology" among the Orthodox living around them. However, as Geertz

---

[3] Bekele and Alemu were respectively clerk of Wereda 24, Kebelle 15 and chairperson of Wereda 23, Kebelle 16. The two men were interviewed for information about their urban precincts.

notes, such findings may also serve as the basis of hypotheses which can then be tested more broadly.

> Anthropologists are not (or, to be more candid, not any longer) attempting to substitute parochial understandings for comprehensive ones, to reduce America to Jonesville or Mexico to Yucatan. They are attempting . . . to discover what contributions parochial understandings can make to comprehensive ones, what leads to general, broad-stroke interpretations particular, intimate findings can produce . . . . But if such insights are to apply to anything beyond those settings, if they are to transcend their parochial origins and achieve a more cosmopolitan relevance, they quite obviously cannot also be validated there. Like all scientific propositions, anthropological interpretations must be tested against the material they are designed to interpret. (Geertz 1968, vii)

Even as anthropologists must conduct narrow descriptive study before they are able to submit theory that can be tested over a much broader arena, so the results of this study serve as an appropriate basis for broader studies on perspectives on the nature of Christ among members of the Ethiopian Orthodox Church.

## Definitions

As noted above, members of the "Ethiopian Orthodox Church" were defined as those identifying themselves as Orthodox Christians when asked to identify their religion. Other key terms to define are "evangelical," "nature" and "person" when referring to Jesus Christ, the offices of the Ethiopian clergy, and terms used to describe the EOC's Christology.

## Evangelical

In this study, the term "evangelical" will be used to designate Christians who believe that God's forgiveness of sin is received through faith in Christ, his death, and resurrection and who believe that they have personally received God's forgiveness by personally trusting or receiving Christ (Erickson 1985). Some Ethiopians understand "evangelical" to refer to a particular Protestant denomination in Ethiopia, the Ethiopian Evangelical Church Mekane Yesus, related to the Lutheran World Federation. Others understand the term to refer to the specific Protestant denominations that are a part of the Evangelical Churches' Fellowship of Ethiopia. In this study, however, the term will be used as synonymous with the term *"penti"* used among most people in Addis Ababa. *"Penti"* is an abbreviation for the English word "pentecostal," but does not necessarily imply someone with a distinctly pentecostal theology of the Holy Spirit. Rather, *pentis* are understood as non-Catholic, non-Ethiopian Orthodox Christians who accept the sufficiency of faith in Christ to obtain forgiveness of sins, particularly as opposed to seeking to earn God's favor or forgiveness through good works or the mediation of *amelajoch*.[4] Many members of the EOC view

---

[4] The *amelajoch* are the many saints and angels who intercede to God on behalf of living Christians who honor them or bring their requests to them. There has been some disagreement as to what is the best English translation of the Amharic word *amelaj* (plural: *amelajoch*). The word is used to describe those who intercede to God on behalf of human beings, and who therefore stand as mediators between God and people.

evangelicals and other Christians who are not Ethiopian Orthodox, such as Catholics, with "suspicion as representatives of alien and heretical creeds" (Ephraim 1971, 267).

## "Nature" and "Person" of Christ

The terms "nature" and "person" are English translations of Greek words used in the Chalcedonian Creed to define the way deity and humanity came together in Jesus Christ. Tesfazghi (1973, 21-48) points out that in Ge'ez (the official church language of Ethiopia) and Amharic (Ethiopia's national language and the language most commonly spoken in the Alert/Gebre Kristos neighborhood of Addis Ababa) there are three words which can mean something similar to the English and Greek words for "nature," all of which also imply the concept of an individual "person." In general, "nature" will be used to describe the essential attribute, character and being of someone, and the word "person" will be used to describe an autonomous, individual personality. However, as different languages will be used throughout the thesis, during the description of the ethnographic method and findings and during the theological evaluation of those findings, the

---

Leslau gives the meaning as both "intercessor" and "mediator," and the word does seem to have at least some connotation of those who intercede because they stand between (Leslau 1976, 17). A number of subjects described an *amelaj* as like a guard through whom a person has to go in order to see another person who is in authority. In this paper the translation "intercessor-mediator" will be used to reflect the field of meaning encompassed by the word.

particular word and language will be specified when the words "nature" or "person" are used.

## Priest, Monk, *Debtara*, Deacon

Levine's (1965) and Ephraim's (1971) definitions of the offices of priest, monk, and *debtara* in the Ethiopian Orthodox Church will be used for this research. The *priests* are the ordained clergy who perform most of the rituals of the church and who obtain status through their proximity to the holy objects of the church itself, particularly the holy ark (*tabot*).[5] Priests may live a worldly lifestyle, but they are still highly regarded simply because they serve God in a holy place. They are sought for blessings, advice, and confession. The *monks* are priests who do not marry and who may not be actively involved in public ministry to lay people. They obtain status through their ascetic pietism and often live as hermits, begging for their food, mortifying their bodies and spending all of their time in prayer and meditation.

The *debtara* have received the education of a priest (and often a great deal more) but are not ordained as priests. Indeed, they may even be defrocked priests. Nevertheless, they have a great deal of status because of their esoteric knowledge. The debtara is an office which does not have a Western equivalent. The debtara is not expected to live a moral life and may even dabble in occultic arts. Yet he

---

[5] See the Glossary of Commonly Used Amharic Terms.

serves the parish as cantor and teacher, and knows the many ancient, holy books associated with the Orthodox church, giving him a great deal of spiritual, mystical power. He puts his knowledge to work for the church, but may also use it to help people obtain special favors, such as helping a woman have a child or helping a man get a job.

Deacons are priests or monks in training. They generally assume the office of deacon at the age of twenty and spend ten years studying the holy books of the church and learning its liturgy and traditions. At the age of thirty, they choose whether to marry and become a priest or remain unmarried and become a monk. At the Gebre Kristos church, the deacons had generally received more formal education than the other clergy; the researcher was often referred to these young men as those who were most knowledgeable of the theology of the church. During the year in which interviews were conducted, one of the deacons reached the age of thirty and became both a priest and a *meri-gaeta*, or a high level of formal theological education, such as a "doctor of theology."

"Monophysite" and "Non-Chalcedonian"

The Council of Chalcedon (A.D. 451) defined Christ as having two natures united in one person, each nature remaining distinct from the other but without separation from the other. Churches throughout the fifth century Christian world which rejected this formula have traditionally been known as "monophysite," taken from the Greek words (μονο-φυσις) for "one nature." The Ethiopian Orthodox Church has usually been characterized as one of these monophysite churches (Frend 1972, 304-308).

However the Ethiopian Orthodox themselves do not accept the term "monophysite" to describe their church. Because Christ was "out of" two natures which united into one composite nature, the EOC rejects the term "monophysite" in favor of the term "*miaphysis*," "mia standing for a composite unity unlike *mone* standing for an elemental unity." The Ethiopian Orthodox prefer to use the expression "non-Chalcedonian Orthodox Churches" for churches which rejected the Council of Chalcedon and hold to a "one nature" Christology (Aymro and Joachim 1970, 97-100).

In general, then, the term "non-Chalcedonian" will be used throughout this paper to describe the Christology of the Ethiopian Orthodox Church, a theology which has traditionally been known as "monophysite." When referring to sources which use the word "monophysite," however, or when referring to ideas which are genuinely monophysite, "monophysite" will be used.

## Overview of the Procedure

To provide background to the ethnographic research, historical, formal, and linguistics perspectives on the nature of Christ in the Ethiopian Orthodox Church were examined from available literature. The results of this examination provide the context for the ethnographic study; these results are summarized in Chapter 3.

The methodology for the ethnographic study is explained in Chapter 4. The researcher conducted fifty-one ethnographic interviews with subjects from the Alert/Gebre Kristos neighborhood of Addis Ababa who identified themselves as Ethiopian Orthodox Christians to determine their perspective on the nature of Christ. Of those interviewed, nineteen were laymen and nineteen were laywomen. Thirteen of those interviewed were members of the clergy.[6] Five clergy identified themselves as priests, three as deacons, two as monks, two as *debtara*, and one as both priest and teacher. Of the fifty-one people interviewed, thirty-seven were not known to the interviewer prior to the interview. The results of these interviews were collected in field notes. The field notes were analyzed for patterns which were grouped and coded using the Ethnograph computer program according to guidelines suggested by Spradley (1979) and Fetterman (1989). The findings are presented in a descriptive, ethnographic report in Chapter 5 which summarizes the subjects' own understanding of the nature of Christ.

Before drawing conclusions based on the findings, a framework for evaluation was established. Chapter 6 is a summary of the theological framework against which the

---

[6]All formally ordained members of the clergy in the EOC are male.

findings have been evaluated. The theological framework includes both the contextual nature of theology and a contemporary statement of Chalcedonian Christology against which EOC Christology can be compared.

In Chapter 7 the findings have been evaluated from several perspectives. First, popular perspectives on the nature of Christ have been analyzed, including comparison with official and linguistic perspectives on the nature of Christ. Second, theological and missiological questions in the Ethiopian context have been considered based on the findings. Third, broader implications for the process of contextual theologizing have been drawn. Finally, areas for further study have been suggested.

# CHAPTER 2
# LITERATURE REVIEW

Research into perceptions of Christ's nature in the Ethiopian Orthodox Church must, of course, begin with an examination of the literature on the history, theology and theological terms of the Ethiopian Orthodox Church. Second, a theological framework must also be established for evaluating perspectives of Christ in the Orthodox Church. Finally, a literature base must be established for the research methodology in history and ethnography which has been followed.

## History, Theology and Theological Terms of the Ethiopian Orthodox Church

In order to understand popular perspectives on the nature of Christ in the Ethiopian Orthodox Church both the history of the doctrine and the present, official statement of the doctrine must be examined. Valuable background on the relationship of the church to Ethiopian society, particularly in the northern areas which are the Church's stronghold, is found in Messing (1957), Reminick (1973) and particularly Levine (1964, 1965, 1972). In addition, Levine (1965), Teshager (1959), Ephraim (1971) and Imbakom (1970) describe the nature of traditional religious education which Ethiopian clergy and laypersons receive, and an article in the Addis Ababa *Monitor* (1995) confirms that such traditional practices were still being used in Addis Ababa in the 1990s. Information on religious education has provided background for the selection of subjects and questions for the ethnographic interviews. Ephraim (1971) is also a good introduction to many aspects of the history, theology and structure of the Ethiopian Orthodox Church and its role in Ethiopian society. In particular, he responds to some of Levine's most controversial observations on Ethiopian society, and should be consulted by anyone using Levine as a introduction to the study of Ethiopia. Shenk (1988) is the best introduction to the question of whether the EOC's deep rootedness in traditional culture has led to a syncretistic or indigenized theology.

## History of the Nature of Christ in the Ethiopian Orthodox Church

Ethiopian studies enjoy a long and distinguished history, and the focus of much research into Ethiopia has been the history of the Ethiopian Orthodox Church (EOC). For example, Jones and Monroe's (1935) standard history of Ethiopia includes extensive discussion of the history of the EOC. The readable style of this older work makes it a good starting place for exploring the background of the specific events in the history of the Ethiopian church.

Bonk (1972) is an indispensable beginning to any study of the Ethiopian Orthodox Church. He divides the study of the church into sections covering its history, theology, literature and art. Though he does not cover the most recent scholarship, there are few older sources in English which he overlooks.

Two older, secondary works, in particular, demand the attention of any student of the Ethiopian Orthodox Church. Blyth (1935) is brief, but accurate, and still provides an adequate introduction for the reader unfamiliar with Ethiopian church history. Far more detailed is Hyatt (1928), based directly on original sources and one of the first comprehensive histories and explanations of the church for a Western audience. Most of Hyatt's material on the ancient and medieval periods has not been supplanted by any more recent work from the Western perspective. Sergew (1970) contains brief essays by the best Ethiopian scholars on both the history and present theology of the church. These essays provide an Ethiopian interpretation which balances the perspective of the fuller European accounts.

Because of the prominence of the EOC throughout the history of the country, histories of particular periods of Ethiopian history inevitably focus on the Church. Sergew's (1972) study is the most in-depth treatment of ancient and early medieval Ethiopian history, and gives detailed treatment of the church from its earliest days until the re-emergence of the Solomonic dynasty (A.D. 1270). Taddesse (1972) includes a detailed study of the history of the church in the late Medieval period, particularly the close relationship of church and state during the expansion of the Ethiopian empire and the evangelization of central Ethiopia. The role of the "monastic holy men" in this evangelization is carefully studied by Kaplan (1984), who traces much of the syncretism in the modern EOC to the evangelistic methods of these holy men and the way the population perceived them. Sergew (1972), Taddesse (1972) and Kaplan (1984) are indispensable sources to understanding the world view of the EOC just prior to the coming of the Jesuits in the sixteenth and seventeenth centuries.

The potentially confusing arguments over the anointing of Christ in the seventeenth through nineteenth centuries are clearly explained by Aren (1978), Bahru (1991) and especially Crummey (1972). The theologies of Christ's anointing that developed during these centuries provide important insight into how the Orthodox understand the nature of Christ today, particularly because they are unique to the Ethiopian context.

Frend (1972) is the place to begin any study of the rise of monophysitism and other non-Chalcedonian Christologies. He skillfully describes the political and theological background to the Council of Chalcedon (A.D. 451) and its aftermath. Frend demonstrates that the rise of non-Chalcedonian Christology was largely a theological phenomena, and was not primarily rooted in the nationalistic impulses of the eastern provinces of the Byzantine Empire. Consequently, to understand any non-Chalcedonian church, one must understand the theology of Cyril, Dioscorus, and Severus. On the other hand, non-Chalcedonian Christologies quickly became identified with the national churches of the countries that embraced it, and it soon became impossible to separate non-Chalcedonian theology from the national identity of non-Chalcedonian churches. Both Chalcedonian and non-Chalcedonian Christologies were firmly rooted in the historical, political and cultural contexts in which they arose. Frend credits Ethiopia's non-Chalcedonian roots to the country's "falling within an Alexandrian sphere of influence" and to the evangelistic work of the nine saints, "individual monks from Syria and Egypt pledged to the anti-Chalcedonian cause" (Frend 1972, 307). Pelikan (1971), Erickson (1991) and Grillmeier (1995) supplement Frend in analyzing how such strongly opposed theologies grew out of the common Nicean tradition.

The most thorough history of the development of non-Chalcedonian Christology in the Ethiopian Orthodox Church is Brake (1973). Beginning with the founding of Christianity in Ethiopia, Brake gives a careful chronological account of every development in the church that affected its non-Chalcedonian theology. He maintains that the church never diverted from its non-Chalcedonian roots. The conflicts with the Jesuits in the sixteenth and seventeenth centuries demonstrated and deepened the church's commitment to non-Chalcedonian theology and forced it to more precisely define its position. The internal debates which began in the seventeenth century accomplished this more precise definition, and further deepened the church's non-Chalcedonian Christology. Brake's study is almost exclusively historical, and his concluding criticism of Ethiopian Orthodox "monophysitism" shows little sensitivity to the issues of contextualized theology. One of the purposes of this thesis is to provide a more adequate response.

Ludolphus (1681) gives one of the most valuable primary sources on the Orthodox Church's conflict with the Jesuits in the sixteenth and seventeenth centuries. Much of his second volume is a report of the events leading up to (what was for him) the recent expulsion of the Jesuits and his own perspective on why they had been forced to leave. Another lengthy, primary source is Geddes (1696) who, along with Budge (1928), quotes the full translated text of a number of important primary documents in Ethiopian church history. Geddes' own conclusions, however, are marked by an anti-Catholic bias and inaccurate generalizations about the EOC's theology. Jowett's (1824) full citation of a letter from the Alexandrian Patriarch to the EOC in the early nineteenth century is important for clarifying the various positions on the anointing of Christ.

## Formal Theology of the Nature of Christ in the Ethiopian Orthodox Church

Much of the theology of the Ethiopian Orthodox Church has developed in the form of debates and arguments, only a few of which have been reduced to writing. When theologies have been written, they have tended to be individual, polemical arguments directed at a particular person or a specific issue rather than comprehensive summaries of doctrine. One of the earliest English summaries of Church's theology is Matthew (1936), a formal response to questions submitted to the church by a relative of the British ambassador to Ethiopia. The entire document is dated, the introduction contains occasional inaccuracies, and the section on the nature of Christ is disappointingly brief. Nevertheless, it does provide a glimpse of the Church's official teaching in the first part of the twentieth century, reflecting the Church's non-Chalcedonian stand after its internal debates on the anointing of Christ.

More recently, however, the EOC and its scholars have made a serious effort to summarize their teachings, and some of these works are available in English. Aymro and Joachim (1970) is brief but clear, and gives a particularly thorough statement of the church's stand on the monophysite-dyophysite controversy. They are often quoted in other works; their book is probably the best introductory work in English for anyone wishing to understand recent EOC theology and practice. Yeshaq (1989) is primarily interested in explaining the church to Westerners, and so concentrates on the history and organization of the church in the Western world. Nevertheless, he does provide an overview of church history from an Ethiopian perspective and gives a complete, clear statement of the church's non-Chalcedonian position.

Similar to Aymro and Joachim, but more recent and less complete, is a work produced by twenty-two of the EOC's archbishops and scholars (Mekarios and others, 1996). The book was written in Amharic, translated into English, and is published in both languages; it is a statement of faith the EOC wishes to disseminate both among is own members and to the outside world. The statement of the Church's perspective on the nature of Christ is much briefer than Aymro and Joachim, but it contains an overview of Ethiopian church history from the Church's official perspective, including a very valuable discussion of the EOC's past and present response to Chalcedon. Mekarios corrects Eadie's (1973) overly optimistic perspective that the Christological differences between the EOC and Chalcedonian churches might soon be bridged. The presence of both Amharic and English text in Mekarios and EOTCHS (1983) is also useful in comparing Amharic and English theological terminology used by the EOC.[1]

---

[1] The published "author" of <u>YeIteyopeya ortodoks tewahedo beite krestiyan acher yetarik yehaymanotena yeserat metsehaf</u> [A short history, faith and order of the Ethiopian orthodox tewahedo church], is the Ethiopian Orthodox Tewahedo Church Holy Synod, abbreviated throughout as EOTCHS.

Four of the most detailed explanations of the church's understanding of the nature of Christ are Poladian (1964), Habte (1964-65), Ayala (1981), and Tesfazghi (1973). Poladian's work was published as an approved, detailed statement of the church's position. He forcefully argues that the "two nature" position of Chalcedon inevitably leads to a division of Christ into two persons. His argument is a challenge to dyophysites to consider whether they have carefully considered the implications of their position. Habte's work is very similar to the sections on Christology in Aymro and Joachim. Like Yeshaq, he is writing to a Western audience, and argues that the EOC position is fundamentally similar to the view of the Western churches. His explanations of the *Qebat* and *Tsegga Lej* positions, however, are simplistic and seem to somewhat misrepresent the *Qebat* position.[2]

Ayala and Tesfazghi are both Ethiopian/Eritrean Catholics. Ayala (1981) is an English translation and revision of an his 1956 Italian (<u>La Chiesa Etiopica e la sua Dottrina Cristologica</u>) and 1959 Amharic-language (<u>YeEtiyopia Beit Christian Silla Christos Bahiryat Akalawi Tewahdo Yemetameno Temhert [The teaching believed by the Ethiopian church concerning the personal union of Christ's natures]</u>) works on EOC Christology. Ayala strongly maintains that EOC Christology is identical to Chalcedon in all but terminology, and so Christological differences do not present a barrier to

---

[2]See the Glossary of Amharic Terms.

the EOC being united to Rome. To support his position he advocates some unusual historical interpretations, but his work is important for understanding the Catholic perspective on EOC Christology.

Ayala's Amharic-language book sparked a host of (mostly critical) responses from Ethiopian Orthodox theologians. Many of these responses are summarized and evaluated by Tesfazghi (1973),[3] who also attempts to synthesize many of the polemical tracts and essays written by Ethiopian Orthodox theologians to one another. His work covers many important issues: Amharic and Ge'ez terms used in Christological discussion, a history of the early debate between the Catholics and the Ethiopian Orthodox on whether Christ had one nature or two, and a discussion of the recent debate among Ethiopian Orthodox theologians on the anointing of Christ. Tesfazghi demonstrates that one of the greatest Christological interests of Ethiopian Orthodox theologians is how their understanding of the anointing of Christ supports their non-Chalcedonian understanding of his nature. Tesfazghi's work is especially valuable, for he organizes the debate into three periods and then allows Ethiopian theologians to speak for themselves, making accessible to the English reader arguments made in three Ethiopian languages.

---

[3]Though Tesfazghi's book was published before the English-language edition of Ayala's book, Tesfazghi's work was based on, and published after, responses to Ayala's 1959 Amharic-language edition.

Like Ayala, his conclusions reflect his own particular biases: the theology of some sections of the Ethiopian church is very close to the traditional, Chalcedonian theology of the Western church, even though a problem of language forces the EOC theologians to express themselves quite differently.

Tesfazghi's linguistic studies have been supplemented with Wolf Laslau's standard Amharic-English dictionary (1976) and Kidan's (n.d.) somewhat rambling Ge'ez-Amharic grammar and dictionary. Kidan's references to Ge'ez theological terms are longer than most of his other entries and include short quotes from EOC theologians. These entries for words with theological meaning helpfully read like short articles in a theological dictionary.

Earlier works on the nature of Christ in Amharic and Ge'ez by Ethiopian theologians are summarized by Tesfazghi. More recent works include Asarat (1991), Berhanu (1993), and Alemayehu (1995a). Asarat and Berhanu confirm the EOC's continued stress on a non-Chalcedonian, single-nature Christology. Berhanu and Alemayehu (in a 1995 follow-up interview) confirm the difficulty of expressing the concept of "two natures" in Amharic or Ge'ez without also implying "two persons" or a self-contradictory way of thinking.

## Theological Framework for Evaluation

Before historical, formal, linguistic and popular perceptions on the nature of Christ in the Ethiopian Orthodox Church can be evaluated, a theological framework will be established from which they can be analyzed. There will be two parts to this framework. First, the contextual nature of theology will be established. Second, a Christology against which the Orthodox Church's Christology can be compared and contrasted will be stated.

## Theology in Context

The Orthodox Church's perspective on the nature of Christ cannot be evaluated until the contextual nature of theology is understood. Schreiter (1985), Bevans (1985) and Stackhouse (1988) introduce the various approaches which have been taken to contextualized theology. The approach taken in this thesis is similar to what Schreiter and Bevans call the "translation model," and is here referred to as "biblically-centered contextual theology." Other models for contextualization will not be discussed in detail, but biblically-centered contextual theology will be defined by contrasting it with an exegesis centered-model and a context-centered model.

### Other Models of Theologizing

Larkin's (1988) comprehensive hermeneutic and methodology of contextualization represents an exegesis-centered model for contextualized theology. Larkin's work has many strengths: he has a very high view of scriptural authority, he builds a detailed theology of contextualization from Scripture itself, and he gives specific, practical guidelines for contextualization. He correctly contends that the author controls the intended meaning of a text and that meaning can be communicated over linguistic and cultural barriers. He also demonstrates the ability of Scripture to reshape interpreters' preunderstandings in line with the intended message of the text.

Nevertheless, Larkin understates the degree to which authors' forms of communication are shaped by their cultural and historical circumstances and the degree to which readers' culturally conditioned pre-understanding affects their interpretation of the text. Consequently, he gives inadequate attention to how interpreters understand the cultural thought patterns of the Bible, how they evaluate their own preunderstandings, and the degree to which interpreters from different contexts might understand a text *differently* without understanding it *disparately*. Larkin also seems to stretch his data when he maintains that the New Testament authors have a sharp distinction "between interpretation and application, between the meaning of a passage and it's significance" (Larkin 1988, 258). While New Testament writers *do* preserve some distinction between interpretation and application, they do not seem to have the same clear-cut categories that Larkin maintains. Larkin's strong biblicism needs to be balanced with more emphasis on cultural and historical context.[4]

---

[4] For a more complete evaluation of Larkin see Strauss 1990.

The "context-centered" approach to theologizing is represented by those who make context a primary *source* for theology. Though many writers could be chosen who represent this approach, Dickson (1984) and Muzorewa (1985) have been cited because they represent African attempts to develop a methodology for theology in context. Muzorewa surveys the history of African theology; Dickson calls for additional development of African theology, fresh Bible translations, hermeneutical principles which recognize "that there is a cultural continuity between the Bible and African life and thought," and freedom from credal traditions. Though not an Africa theologian, Croatto (1981) has been cited because of his particularly sharp rejection of a biblically-centered paradigm for theologizing. Sawyerr's (1968) suggestion that the Church be understood in Africa as a "Great Family" is an example of a contextual-centered theology in the African context. These context-centered theologies correctly understand the role that context plays in shaping understanding, but they do not place enough emphasis on the unique revelatory nature of Scripture and the way it is normative for people of all contexts. The result is a loss of Scriptural authority as an absolute foundation for theology.

## Biblically-Centered Contextual Theology

The approach to contextual theology taken in this thesis is best represented by Conn, Padilla and Tienou, undergirded by the hermeneutic of Anthony Thiselton. Though he has made a valuable contribution to biblically-centered contextual theology, Charles Kraft's view of Scripture is too deficient for him to be a comprehensive example of this model.

### Primary Contributors: Conn, Padilla, Tienou, and Thiselton

Conn (1978, 1984) uses the interaction between theology and anthropology over the past two hundred years to highlight the issues of contextualization of theology and of theological education. He lists six important criteria for theologizing: biblical-theological, covenantal, culture-specific, confessional, communal, and prophetic. Conn's suggestion that the Bible itself offers the right models for contextual theologizing are valuable, but his implication that the preaching of New Covenant evangelists was primarily a contextualization of Old Covenant truth is incomplete. Though Conn also needs to be clearer on the overall goal of interpretation, he successfully balances the importance of biblical absolutes with the significant role context plays in theologizing.

Padilla (1980) is an outstanding introduction to a hermeneutic of contextual theology. Hermeneutics is "a dialogue between Scripture and the contemporary historical context," and so involves both the interpreter's context and the scriptural context (Padilla 1980, 70). Theology will emerge as a result of this dialogue, and so cannot "be reduced to the repetition of doctrinal formulations borrowed from other latitudes" (Padilla 1980, 73). Padilla gives priority to letting "Scripture speak for itself" as the first step in the dialogue; he preserves the full authority of Scripture while displaying adequate sensitivity to culture. In a subsequent article he calls for a hermeneutic that is communal (though allowing a humble role for professional theologians), pneumatic (though not minimizing grammatical-historical interpretation), contextual (with each church bringing its contextual horizon to the text, even as the early Christians did), and missiological (with the end purpose of theology being outreach; Padilla 1983).

Tienou asks the question: "What do we mean when we say that the Bible is authoritative in our theology?" He affirms "that our understanding of the Bible cannot be separated from our prior questions and concerns" (Tienou 1983, 98). To reach beyond these preunderstandings, theologians must begin with the problems of human existence and examine them in biblical perspective, in a specific cultural milieu, and then seek to correlate the two. Tienou (1984) illustrates this process, as he examines proposals that ecclesiology in Africa could profitably be built on the concept of the church as the great family of God. He responds by cautioning against a mnemic hermeneutic that takes one's own context instead of the Bible as the starting point in constructing a paradigm for understanding the Scriptures. He is especially wary of theologies that include in the family of God ancestors who have not known Christ.

Anthony Thiselton (1977a, 1977b, 1980, 1985, 1992) lays a comprehensive foundation for the theologizing of Conn, Padilla, and Tienou. Thiselton sees hermeneutics as the merging of the horizon of the text with the horizon of the interpreter. Because individuals *always* understand in relation to themselves, interpreters' understanding of the biblical text will always be in relation to their own personal, historical, and cultural context. However this preunderstanding does not mean that interpreters are doomed to simply read their own understandings into texts. Responding to the philosophy of doubt in hermeneutics, Thiselton clearly demonstrates that it is possible for interpreters to adequately, though not exhaustively, understand a text. Indeed, the revelatory nature of biblical texts demands that they extend their horizons and seek to read the text as it was meant to be read, and commonalities among human beings mean that readers from very different contexts can arrive at complementary understandings of the same text. Thiselton's call for a metacritical approach to evaluating interpretations safeguards against any particular reading community twisting the text to simply reinforce its own theological inclinations.

On the Periphery: Kraft

Though Charles Kraft has been identified as a primary example of the translation model of contextualization (Bevans

1985, Schreiter 1985), he must be classified as on the periphery of biblically-centered contextual theology. Kraft rightly affirms the contextual nature of all theology and the importance of inter-cultural theology, and he gives a great deal of emphasis to Scripture. He also stresses the importance of exegesis to read the text as it was first read, the possibility of people from all cultures adequately understanding God's supra-truth in Scripture, the hermeneutical spiral in which the Scripture corrects the thinking of its readers, and the sin-tainted nature of human culture.

However, Kraft's view of Scripture is ultimately inadequate. He sees the Bible as primarily a "case-book" of God's revelation; it is not itself revelation until it is "personalized." He does not put enough emphasis on the progress of revelation in Scripture, and he believes that general revelation is informationally adequate for salvation. Though he offers many very helpful ideas, Kraft's inadequate view of Scripture disqualifies him from being fully classified as a biblically-centered contextual theologian.

Secondary Contributors

Besides Conn, Padilla, Tienou, Thiselton, and Kraft, a number of other theologians and missiologists have made important contributions to the model of biblically-centered contextual theology accepted in this thesis. Sundkler's (1979) article on the future of African theology first appeared in 1960 and was amazingly prophetic. He understands theology as "an ever-renewed re-interpretation to new generations and peoples of the given Gospel" (Sundkler 1979, 493). Sundkler calls for the church in Africa to develop theology especially relevant to its context and to make a contribution to the theology of the universal church.

Another pioneer in the development of contextualized theology is Charles Taber. In the inaugural issue of the short-lived journal <u>Gospel in Context</u>, Taber (1978) emphasizes the cultural conditioning of all theology. He suggests that, in the same way that western theology has used the intellectual tools of philosophy and law to do theology, other cultures should use other conceptual tools in developing a hermeneutic for theologizing. He also calls for non-professionals in the West and for those from the two-thirds world to get involved in the theologizing task.

Hesselgrave and Rommen (1989) and Gilliland (1989) are useful introductions to contextualization. Hesselgrave and Rommen only touch on a number of important questions, but present an excellent summary of a universal frame of conceptual reference, including semantic relationships, which allow communication among peoples of different times and cultures. Gilliland argues for contextual theologizing by the whole church as the best means for incarnational mission "without paternalizing, dominating, or setting up foreign and dependent churches" (Gilliland 1989, 13).

Hundley (1993) deals with all of the major hermeneutical issues that must be resolved in developing a theology and methodology of contextualization. He believes that all presentations of the gospel are contextualized, and skillfully refutes objections to an evangelical approach to contextualization.

Hirsch (1967) often provokes a storm of controversy, but his ideas are fundamentally sound. His hermeneutical model is particularly useful in understanding how people from different contexts can understand a text differently but not disparately. Thiselton, Osborne (1991) and Erickson (1993) provide clarifying balance to Hirsch's thinking on "authorial intent." Osborne's comprehensive guide to biblical hermeneutics further demonstrates the possibility of adequately reading a text the way it was meant to be read through the hermeneutical spiral.

Specific Aspects of Contextualization

Several writers have contributed to particular aspects of biblically-centered contextual theology. Hiebert (1984) and Gration (1984) have both developed practical "how-to" guides to contextual theologizing which isolate issues for which a contextual theology is needed. In many cases these issues are felt-needs which can be brought to the surface by asking questions such as "Where has the gospel not yet been good news to our culture?" (Gration 1984) The result will be that some cultural practices will be retained, some will be discarded, and some will be modified; new symbols and rites will also be created to replace the old (Hiebert 1984).

Cole (1984) and Hiebert (1989) contribute to the distinction between what is absolute and what is relative in contextual theology. Cole draws a contrast between absolute and relative data bases for theologizing. Only the absolute data found in the Scripture carries authority. Hiebert sorts through the difficult relationship of form and meaning in expressing biblical truth and suggests a continuum: some forms are tied very closely to meaning and must be retained, while others are more loosely tied to meaning and may be replaced.

Chang (1981) and Simbo (1983) both call for a greater contribution from the non-Western world in developing a process for theologizing. Chang suggests that hermeneutics itself is affected by the context. While leaving many questions unanswered, he persuasively argues that interpreters may come closer to reading the text the way it was meant to be read if they follow reading strategies not taught in traditional Western theological education. Simbo (1983) notes the Greek, philosophical roots of Western theology. The results have been an accommodating theology that emphasizes the intellectual and theoretical at the expense of addressing real issues of how people should live, and a paternalism in its dealings with other cultures. Many third world cultures are built on thought patterns that are similar to Hebraic thought patterns, and should form the basis for a non-Western contribution to theological method.

Muller (1991) and Lindbeck (1984) have helped define the role of historical theology and the creeds of the church to contextual theology done by contemporary churches. Muller stresses that, because all doctrine is developed within a historical context, faithfulness to the doctrinal statements of the past demands careful understanding of the circumstances surrounding the development of the statement. Lindbeck points out that the differences in historical context mean that faithfulness to doctrine probably will demand a restatement of that doctrine in fresh terms for each new historical situation.

A Christological Framework

It is beyond the scope of this thesis to establish a contemporary Chalcedonian Christology based on first-hand exegesis of Scripture and weighing the considerations of different theologians. Rather the Ethiopian Orthodox perceptions of the nature of Christ will be compared with one contemporary Chalcedonian Christology. Some Western theologians such as Hick (1977, 1993) have hotly disputed the adequacy of Chalcedon, but the debate in the West has generally assumed that Jesus was human and has concentrated its discussion on whether he could also have been God in flesh. Erickson (1991) is a fully developed, contemporary Chalcedonian Christology which interacts with a Western one-nature Christology (Leigh 1982) that is strikingly similar to the EOC's position. Erickson gives an excellent historical survey of the background to and aftermath of Chalcedon itself, followed by a detailed discussion of why Chalcedonian Christology is deemed inadequate by many today. He responds with his own contemporary incarnational Christology which answers the critics and remains faithful to Chalcedon.

## Research Theory and Method

Two kinds of research methodology have shaped this thesis: historical and ethnographic. All historians work within a historiographic framework. Studies in the historical development of Christology in the Ethiopian Orthodox Church must be preceded by an overview of the historiographic framework which has been followed in evaluating the historical data. However the more important research methodology for this thesis has been in ethnography and anthropology. Both a conceptual framework in anthropology and specific methods in ethnographic research have shaped the research procedure for collecting data to evaluate popular perspectives on the nature of Christ.

## Historiographic Method

Carr (1961) lays one of the best foundations for historiographic research. History begins when someone chooses to give significance to a fact from the past; because someone has *chosen* to give significance to that fact, all history is interpretive. First, the data from which historians discover and report facts are colored by the interpretation and the worldview of the people who provided the data. Second, historians themselves are influenced by their own time, society, culture, and motivation for studying a particular part of history. Nevertheless, by being aware of the context which shaped the data and which is shaping them, historians can create working models of the past which enable them to understand it. The Ethiopian church historian must be particularly aware of the political and ecclesiastical pressures that shaped original Ethiopian sources and the ethnocentric biases that shaped original European sources.

Fischer (1970) balances Carr's overly optimistic assessment of the role of historians in verifying their facts. He reminds historians of the many fallacies into which they can fall and provides guidelines that will help them be accurate and objective in collecting their data.

Barzun and Graff's work (1992) is still the most comprehensive theory and practice of historical research available, and has been updated (5th edition) to remain current. They remind the historian that "*no piece of evidence can be used in the state in which it is found*. It must undergo the action of the researcher's mind known as the critical method" (Barzun and Graff 1992, 159; italics original). That action includes generalization and corroboration, two processes developed in detail by Lichtman and French (1978). First, historians need to evaluate their data based on what is generally known about the time, place, people, society, values, and ideas of what is being studied.

> Only by drawing on his knowledge of how people are likely to behave and how the world works, can the historian make arguments that enable him to reconstruct the past, to determine what happened. (Lichtman and French 1978, 16)

Second, historians need to seek further evidence, particularly from other sources, that will support the data.

> Whenever possible, historians try to corroborate the account of any witness by searching for other evidence that helps them to choose among competing reports of the events being described. (Lichtman and French 1978, 29)

In a study of Ethiopian church history, such generalization and corroboration has been done primarily by comparing Ethiopian and European sources to get a balanced perspective of what actually took place.

## Anthropological Framework and Ethnographic Research Methodology

In order to do research into present, popular perspectives on the nature of Christ among Ethiopian Orthodox, both a anthropological framework and specific guidelines for conducting ethnographic research are necessary.

### Anthropological Framework

The anthropological framework for evaluating popular perspectives on the nature of Christ has been provided by Clifford Geertz (1968, 1973, 1983, 1988). Geertz describes the process of understanding other cultures "from the native's point of view" as a "thick description" of the significant symbols of their culture (Geertz 1983, 56-57). Thick description must be "actor-oriented," focusing on how people themselves describe and explain the symbols and events in their culture (Geertz 1973, 14). It does not pretend to be comprehensive or exhaustive, but rather informs "guesses at meanings" which are assessed in order to shape better guesses (Geertz 1973, 20).

> The aim is to draw large conclusions from small, but densely textured facts; to support broad assertions about the role of culture in the construction of collective life by engaging them exactly with complex specifics. (Geertz 1973, 28)

Thick description of religious symbols is particularly important because "sacred symbols function to synthesize a people's ethos . . . and their world view" (Geertz 1973, 89). For any group of people, religious symbols are models of reality and for reality. They give meaning to "reality both by shaping themselves to it and by shaping it to themselves" (Geertz 1973, 93). Sacred symbols connect the "is" and the "ought"--the ontology and ethics--of life and so provide the key to understanding a people's world view.

One of the most significant symbols of the Ethiopian Orthodox Church is its understanding of the "one nature" of Christ. The focus of the present research has been a thick description of the way members of the Orthodox Church themselves explain their understanding of the nature of Christ. Geertz asserts that thick description done of a particular group of people in a particular location forms the basis of theory which can then be tested in the wider arena of life (Geertz 1968, vii). Thick description of how one group of Ethiopian Orthodox understand the nature of Christ will provide a basis for wider research and conclusions on popular Orthodox Christology and for missiological approaches among the particular group of people researched.

Geertz's approach provides a means of genuinely (if not exhaustively) understanding people of another culture without trying to get inside their minds to think the same thoughts that they think (Geertz 1983, 56-57). It reflects a deep respect for cultures and worldviews other than ones own. Finally, Geertz (1968) demonstrates how history can support ethnography by contributing to thick description, especially in religious matters. A historical survey of Christological development is an important part of understanding present perspectives on the nature of Christ in the Ethiopian Orthodox Church.

## Ethnographic Research Methodology

The primary research tool for developing a thick description of Ethiopian Orthodox perspectives on the nature of Christ has been qualitative, ethnographic interviews. Guidelines for developing qualitative, descriptive, ethnographic research have been described by Fetterman (1989), Spradley (1979) and Marshall and Rossman (1989). Marshall and Rossman point out the value of such a qualitative study.

> The strengths of qualitative studies should be demonstrated for research that is exploratory or descriptive and that stresses the importance of context, setting, and subjects' frame of reference. (Marshall and Rossman 1989, 46)

The purpose of the present research has been to explore, probe, and describe how Ethiopian Orthodox believers *actually* express their understanding of the nature of Christ. The primary tool has been "qualitative, in-depth interviews," which, as Marshall and Rossman explain,

> are more like conversations than formal, structured interviews. The researcher explores a few general topics to help uncover the participant's meaning perspectives, but otherwise respects how the participant names and structures the responses. This, in fact, is an assumption fundamental to qualitative research--the participant's perspective on the social phenomenon of interest should unfold as the participant views it, not as the researcher views it. (Marshall and Rossman 1989, 82)

The present research has been an attempt to use ethnographic questions in in-depth interviews to allow participants' views on the nature of Christ to emerge.

Spradley (1989) develops a detailed taxonomy of ethnographic questions which allow researcher's to establish and explore their subjects' own frame of reference. The questions include descriptive questions which collect subjects' own vocabulary and determine what is truly important to them, structural questions which expand, narrow, and verify the researchers' emerging hypotheses, and contrast questions which allow more in-depth analysis.

Guidelines for selecting subjects have been taken from Fetterman (1989) and from Monette, Sullivan and DeJong (1990).

Monette, Sullivan and DeJong discuss "nonprobability sampling," which involves selection of subjects when claims of representativeness are less important. Nonprobability sampling includes availability sampling, snowball sampling, quota sampling, purposive sampling, and dimensional sampling (Monette, Sullivan and DeJong 1990, 150-56). Principles from all these sampling methods have been used in the selection of subjects for the present research. These techniques have been combined in what Fetterman describes as "stratified judgmental sampling," in which researchers rely on their judgment to select appropriate subjects based on the research question being asked (Fetterman 1989, 43; 99). Such sampling is not based on true random sampling techniques, but the research question at hand does not require truly random sample.

Principles for analyzing the results of then ethnographic interviews have come primarily from Fetterman (1989) and from Bogden and Bilken (1982). Bogden and Bilken encourage a narrowing of the focus of research based on results of early interviews and the recording of "observer's comments" as ideas are generated during the research process. They also develop a system of coding interviews based on ideas that are repeated by subjects within the context of the research interest (Bogden and Bilken 1982, 154-67).

Fetterman provides several helpful tools for analysis. First, he introduces the important analytical concept of "triangulation." Triangulation is "testing one source of information against another to strip away alternative explanations and prove a hypothesis" (Fetterman 1989, 89). Triangulation can be implemented by comparing the official and unofficial remarks of a single subject, by comparing different subjects, by comparing the comments of subjects with the comments of individuals who are not subjects, and by comparing all other data with written information. "The trick is to compare comparable items and levels during analysis" (Fetterman 1989, 90).

Fetterman's second analytical tool is observation of patterns. Researchers should compare, contrast, and sort "gross categories and minutiae until a discernible thought or behavior becomes identifiable" (Fetterman 1989, 92). From these thoughts or behaviors, researchers should construct an initial "poorly defined model" which they should then test against other data. As variations and exceptions emerge, the hypothesis is altered, and researchers begin to see patterns emerge. Because "any cultural group's patterns of thoughts and behavior are interwoven strands," discovery of one pattern will lead researchers to other patterns (Fetterman 1989, 92). By "mixing and matching" the emerging patterns researchers begin to build theory. Researchers will continue the spiral of comparing theory with data until "a convergence of similarities" results in the crystallization of conclusions about reality.

> Every study has classic moments when everything falls into place . . . . All the subtopics, miniexperiments, layers

> of triangulated effort, key events, and patterns of behavior form a coherent and often cogent picture of what is happening. (Fetterman 1989, 101)

Full crystallization of thought often does not come until researchers begin to write up the results of their research (Fetterman 1989, 105).

# CHAPTER 3
# THE CONTEXT: HISTORICAL, FORMAL, AND LINGUISTICS PERSPECTIVES ON THE NATURE OF CHRIST IN THE ETHIOPIAN ORTHODOX CHURCH

Over the centuries, non-Chalcedonian Christology has become one of the most important defining points of the Ethiopian Orthodox Church (EOC), distinguishing it from Western Christianity. Consequently, the doctrine has far-reaching implication for the process of doing theology and missions in Ethiopia. To appreciate the significance of the EOC's "one nature" Christology and the need to understand popular perspectives on the nature of Christ among Orthodox believers, however, one must understand the historical development of the doctrine, the church's formal teaching about the nature of Christ, and the terminology used in the Amharic and Ge'ez languages to describe the nature of Christ.

## Historical Perspectives on the Nature of Christ in the Ethiopian Orthodox Church

The development of Christology in the Ethiopian Orthodox Church can be divided into three different stages: the establishment of non-Chalcedonian Christianity in Ethiopia, Orthodoxy's clash with western Christology as introduced by the Jesuits, and Orthodoxy's internal debates over the anointing of Christ.

## The Establishment of Non-Chalcedonian Christianity in Ethiopia

From it earliest years, the church in Ethiopia was closely connected with the Church of Alexandria. When the Alexandrian and other eastern churches rejected the Council of Chalcedon and followed a different understanding of the nature of Christ, the Church of Ethiopia stayed allied with her mother church in Egypt. Subsequent missionary activity from several non-Chalcedonian churches tied the church in Ethiopia even more tightly to the non-Chalcedonian position.

### Christianity Comes to Ethiopia

Rufinius of Tyre (d. A.D. 410) tells the story of the founding of Christianity in Ethiopia.[1] A philosopher from Tyre named Meripius was traveling to India when his ship was forced to stop for supplies on the southwestern shores of the Red Sea in what is now Eritrea. The local inhabitants were hostile to the Roman Empire at the time,[2] and killed everyone on the ship except two boys, Frumentius and Aidesius. They sold the boys as slaves to the highland Ethiopians, and they eventually came to serve the king of the country. Frumentius

---

[1] Rufinius' account is related by many historians. The account recorded here is the one presented by Jones and Monroe, 26-31.

[2] Though Sergew insists that the Axumites were on good terms with the Romans at this time (Sergew 1972, 100).

became his secretary and Aidesius served as his cupbearer. When the king died, the queen asked the two young men to assist in raising her son. The boys were Christians, and they took advantage of their high position to promote their faith, encouraging the Roman merchants in the Ethiopian capital of Axum to build Christian prayer houses. When the king had grown, he allowed the boys to go free. Aidesius returned to Tyre, but Frumentius went to Alexandria. He received an audience with Athanasius and encouraged him to appoint a bishop for Ethiopia who would promote mission work there. Athanasius responded by appointing Frumentius himself, who returned to Ethiopia and spread the Christian faith. Rufinius' story is confirmed by coins during the reign of the Ethiopian king Ezana, which show that he became a Christian during his reign, and by a letter from the Roman Emperor Constantius in 356 to his "precious brothers" Ezana and Shaizana in Ethiopia.

Constantius' letter (Sergew 1972, 101-2) also demonstrates the strong ties which developed between the church of Ethiopia and the church of Egypt. Because of Constantius' sympathy toward Arianism, he had deposed Athanasius, and he was writing to the king of Ethiopia to demand that Frumentius be sent back to the Roman Empire so that his theology could be examined by the new bishop of Alexandria. There is no indication that the Ethiopian Emperor Ezana had any inclination to obey the demands of the distant emperor of Rome. Rather, the high esteem with which Frumentius has always been held in Ethiopia and the traditions which affirm that he spent the rest of his life in Ethiopia argue that the king did not send him back to Egypt. This incident set a pattern for the Ethiopian church: rather than passively following the lead of the western church, the church of Ethiopia would tenaciously cling to teachings which it deemed were true to the traditions of its founders.

## The Origin of Chalcedonian and Monophysite Christologies

During the fourth and fifth centuries the church in the eastern Mediterranean was torn apart with conflicts over the nature of Christ. The issue was vitally important to even the most common Christians because they were taught that their eternal salvation depended on correct belief concerning Christ's deity and humanity. For example, Apollinarius taught that if Christ was in any sense merely a man, "he would have no salvation to bestow," and to say he had a human nature which was distinct from his divine nature was to make a part of him merely man (Frend 1972, 116). Apollinarius, therefore, stressed that "the human flesh of Christ was, from the moment of conception, joined with the Godhead in an absolute oneness of being; consequently Christ's flesh, became glorified, divine, and immortal and shared "the names and properties of the Word, and vice versa" (Erickson 1991, 60-61).

Cyril and Nestorius

Apollinarius' teachings were rejected at the Council of Constantinople (A.D. 381) because they made Jesus something other than truly human. However the debate was soon resumed by Cyril, Bishop of Alexandria, and Nestorius, Bishop of Constantinople. Nestorius emphasized the completeness of Christ's humanity by stressing the duality of his human and divine natures. To show the distinctiveness of Christ's two natures, Nestorius claimed that the Virgin Mary could not have been *theotokos* ("God-bearer"), but only *Christotokos* ("Christ-bearer"), because Mary gave birth only to Christ's humanity. God could not have a mother, and in the same way that God could not be born, neither could God suffer and die.

Nestorius' strong language opened the door for his opponents, particularly Cyril, to suggest that Nestorius was teaching that Christ's two natures were united only by a single will, and so that he was "actually two distinct persons, one divine and one human" (Erickson 1991, 63; Frend 1972, 18).[3] Cyril accepted Christ's full humanity, but insisted that his human and divine natures combined into a single nature which always acted as a unity. To say that Christ acted at times as only a human being and at times as

---

[3]There is considerable debate as to whether Nestorius actually held to the theological position which was ultimately attributed to him. It is clear, however, that there were those who held to the position that was ultimately condemned as "Nestorianism." This name will be retained as a useful label for that position (Erickson 1991, 62).

only God would divide the person of Christ into two, jeopardizing mankind's salvation. If only a man suffered and died, then Christ could not be savior of the Cosmos. The eternal Logos himself, and not just a man assumed by the Logos, had to be born of a woman and be crucified; otherwise salvation would not bring the gift of immortality (Pelikan 1971, 234). Therefore it must never be said that Christ was born, suffered, died, or did anything else only in his humanity (Pelikan 1971, 245-47).[4] Though Christ might display differences in his humanity and deity, there could be no division between the two. Christ was "one person with one nature which possessed the attributes of deity and humanity without the transferring of the properties of either to the other" (Brake 1977, 22).

The debate between Nestorius and Cyril climaxed at the Council of Ephesus (A.D. 431), when Nestorius was condemned. Two years later a "Formula of Reunion" united the Alexandrian church, which had supported Cyril, and the Antiochene church, which had supported Nestorius, by saying that Christ was "of two natures" "in a union without confusion" (Frend 1972, 21). However the issue was not fully decided. The Alexandrians felt that the Formula of Reunion did not adequately protect the united person of Christ, and many of the Antiochenes felt

---

[4]Pelikan also points out that the battle against the Arian, Gnostic, and docetic heresies led to the fear that speaking of Christ as acting only in his humanity would ultimately destroy the perfect deity of Christ.

the condemnation of Nestorius had been too harsh. When Cyril died in A.D. 444, his successor, Dioscorus, began to attack the two nature formula. An aged monk from Constantinople, Eutyches, went further: he taught that when Christ's divinity and humanity united, his two natures fused into one nature. He seems to have also concluded that Christ's humanity was swallowed up by his divinity, making his flesh no longer human flesh, "but the flesh of the Word incarnate" (Frend 1972, 30), a position similar to Apollinarianism.[5]

## The Council of Chalcedon

When the archbishop of Constantinople, Flavian, requested that Pope Leo of Rome express his opinion on the issue of Christ's deity and humanity, Leo penned his famous *Tome* stating that Christ's distinct human and divine natures were united in one person, without confusion. But when Eutyches' views were examined by the "Robber Synod" of Ephesus (A.D. 449), Dioscorus was in control and would not allow the *Tome* to be read. The Synod exonerated Eutyches. However, in the summer of 450 the Emperor Theodosius died, and his sister, Pulcheria, came to the throne in Constantinople. She and her new husband, Marcian, favored Leo's position, and so called the Council of Chalcedon in an attempt to finally decide the issue and unite the church (A.D. 451). The Council condemned

---

[5]Like Nestorius, Eutyches' views have been passed down through others, and it is difficult to determine what the man himself actually taught.

both Eutyches and Nestorius and accepted the *Tome of Pope Leo*, stating that Christ had

> two natures, *inconfusedly, unchangedably, indivisibly, inseparably;* the distinction of the natures being by no means taken away by the union, but rather the property of each nature being preserved, and concurring in one Person (*prosôpon*) and one Subsistence (*hypostasis*), not parted or divided into two persons, but one and the same Son. (Schaff 1877, 62)

Though it may seem that Chalcedon settled the matter, many who were present did not regard the council's conclusion as a Symbol of Faith with the same status as the more ancient creeds or the teachings of the church Fathers (Frend 1972, 48). In the West, the Council was given the status of "a binding document and a definition of faith which was not susceptible to negotiation," but in the East, it was immediately attacked (Frend 1972, 49). Riots broke out in Alexandria (Frend 1972, 149), and Dioscorus responded that the perfect union of Christ's human and divine natures gave him a human nature that was "quite different from ours" and "declared that it would be profane to consider the blood of Christ to be natural" (Erickson 1991, 68). A generation later, Severus, patriarch of Antioch, advanced a more mild position. He insisted that "Word and flesh did retain their 'properties'" (Frend 1972, 212), and attacked those who taught that Christ's deity had absorbed his humanity. But he also felt that Chalcedon led to a disunity in Christ's life because it allowed one to speak of Christ "performing human acts in his human nature and divine acts in his divine nature"

(Erickson 1991, 69). Severus emphasized that Christ's two natures became one in the incarnation and that all of Christ's acts, "God-befitting and man-befitting were those of one Christ," a unified person, with a single divine-human nature (Frend 1972, 209; see also Grillmeier 1995, 33).

Though Apollinarian and Eutychian monophysitism would persist, the more moderate theology of Cyril and Severus would become the foundation for the great non-Chalcedonian movement which soon controlled Egypt and Syria. In the hundred years following Chalcedon, a separate, non-Chalcedonian ecclesiastical hierarchy gradually developed throughout the East. Furthermore, the zeal of the non-Chalcedonian theologians to preserve and spread their Christology led them to aggressive missionary activity in Nubia, Armenia, and Ethiopia, establishing each of these as a "monophysite kingdom" (Frend 1972, 296-315).[6]

## Non-Chalcedonian Christology Established in Ethiopia

The close connection between the Ethiopian church and the Egyptian church makes it "reasonable to suppose that from the beginning in matters of dogma the Ethiopian Church was on the side of the Alexandrian Patriarch who opposed the

---

[6]The preferred name for the non-Chalcedonian churches that arose in the East has been "Oriental Orthodox Churches," and, besides the Ethiopian Orthodox Church, includes the Armenian Apostolic Church, the Coptic Orthodox Church of Egypt, the Syrian Orthodox Church in India, and the Syrian Orthodox Patriarchate (Third and fourth consultations 1971, 214).

definition of the Chalcedonian Christological formula" (Sergew 1972, 112; see also Frend 1972, 305). However the EOC's commitment to non-Chalcedonian Christology was sealed in the late fifth century when a group of missionaries, primarily from Syria, came from Byzantium to minister in Ethiopia. These Nine Saints played an important part in extending Christianity throughout the Axsumite Empire and rooting it more deeply in the soil where it already existed. Anti-monophysite persecutions in the Byzantine empire were one of the main reasons the Nine Saints came to Ethiopia, though there is also evidence that they came as part of a program "of careful recruitment and selection by the (Monophysite) patriarchate of Alexandria" to promote non-Chalcedonian Christianity and further solidify its control of Ethiopian ecclesiastical affairs (Tadesse 1972, 23; 29; Sergew 1972, 116; Jones and Monroe 1935, 38). Certainly the Nine Saints' zeal for the non-Chalcedonian understanding of Christ's nature played a major role in establishing non-Chalcedonian Christology in Ethiopia. Besides translating large portions of the Bible into Ge'ez,[7] they also translated several books which teach non-Chalcedonian Christology (the *Qerlos* and the *Decta Fide* of Cyril of Alexandria) and which attack the Nestorians (Jones and Monroe 1955, 35; Brake 1977, 67).

---

[7]Ge'ez, or ancient Ethiopic, is still the language of the Ethiopian Orthodox Church. It is also the foundation of many modern Ethiopian languages, but it is no longer spoken outside of the church.

During the lives of the Nine Saints, non-Chalcedonian Christianity was firmly secured throughout Ethiopia and even spread across the Red Sea to southern Arabia.[8]

The strength of the non-Chalcedonian position in Ethiopia in these early days is evidenced from two incidents which took place soon after the coming of the Nine Saints. Justinian (527-65) of Byzantium tried to reach a uniformed teaching on the nature of Christ with the anti-Chalcedonians. When this failed, however, he exiled the non-Chalcedonian Alexandrian Patriarch, Theodosius, and replaced him with a Chalcedonian named Paul. An Arabic source says that when the Ethiopians heard that the new Patriarch of Alexandria was a Chalcedonian, and when their own "Episcopal Chair" was vacant, they refused to send for a replacement from Alexandria. Instead, they sent a delegation to Justinian requesting that he nominate a bishop who was non-Chalcedonian. When he

---

[8] Ayala argues that there is no evidence that the Nine Saints were non-Chalcedonian (Ayala 1981, 41-45). His only proof, however, is the good relations that existed between the Ethiopian Emperor Kaleb and the Chalcedonian Byzantine Emperor Justinian and the lack of any formal decree from the EOC condemning Chalcedon. However Ayala does not discuss the strong evidence of early non-Chalcedonian thinking in Ethiopia (see below). There are few records of any formal theological pronouncements of the EOC in these early years, and it does not seem unlikely that Chalcedonian and non-Chalcedonian emperors could have had good relations in the face of a common, non-Christian enemy. Ayala's conclusions seem strongly influenced by his desire to demonstrate a theological unity between the EOC and the Catholic Church and to pin the blame for disunion on Alexandria's desire to keep the EOC under its control. His evidence is not strong enough to dismiss the traditional argument that the Nine Saints helped secure non-Chalcedonian Christology in Ethiopia.

refused, the Ethiopians returned without a bishop, and remained without one for twenty-five years, even though this meant it was impossible for priests and deacons to be consecrated. When a Chalcedonian bishop was sent to Ethiopia by Paul, he was put to death. To encourage the Ethiopians in their struggle against Chalcedon, the exiled Theodosius sent Dionysius of Halicornasus to Ethiopia "to support the Christians in their faith" (Sergew 1972, 142).

Another incident which shows the early strength of non-Chalcedonian Christology in Ethiopia comes from John, Bishop of Ephesus. He writes of a certain Longinus who visited Nubia in the late 500s and discovered missionaries from Abyssinia who were teaching that "Christ suffered in a body not capable of pain, or of death" and that he had responded by teaching "the correct belief." Longinus also met Axumites "who professed the teachings of Julian Halicarnassus, who believed that the body of Jesus Christ is incorruptible" (Sergew 1972, 177). A hundred years later a war was fought between Axum and the Chalcedonian Nubian kingdom of Mekuria, at least partially over doctrinal issues, and continued until "the Anti-Chalcedonian group defeated the opposition and imposed its doctrinal teachings on the other" (Sergew 1972, 194). Missionaries preaching more extreme forms of monophysitism in the sixth century and wars fought against Chalcedonian theology in the seventh century demonstrate that the Ethiopian church was firmly committed to non-Chalcedonian Christology from its earliest years.

## Non-Chalcedonian Christology in Ethiopia's "Dark Ages"

Historical data for the development of the church in Ethiopia from 680-1270 is limited, but much of this time was clearly one of struggle. The rise of Islam separated Ethiopia from the West and led to a decline of the Axumite kingdom. During the tenth century a Jewish queen named Yodit ravaged the church. At about the same time, the Ethiopian Orthodox Church had a series of misunderstandings with her mother church in Alexandria over the appointment of the Abuna.[9] A long period followed during which there was no Abuna or bishops in Ethiopia, and, hence, no consecration of priests or deacons.

The doctrine of the nature of Christ seems to have developed very little during this time of struggle, but, as Brake says, "One would not expect a detailed theological debate in a period of struggle for religious existence" (Brake 1977, 86). Brake gives four reasons why it is certain that non-Chalcedonian Christology remained the official teaching of the church. First, for the most part, the Ethiopian Orthodox Church maintained its close ties with the Egyptian church, and the Egyptian church remained non-Chalcedonian. Second, there

---

[9]The Egyptian patriarch appointed the Ethiopian Abuna, or metropolitan, until the twentieth century.

is no historical mention of a departure from non-Chalcedonian Christology. Third, beginning in 1270 (when more numerous historical records are again available in Ethiopia) there are references to the non-Chalcedonian nature of the Ethiopian Orthodox Church, with no indication that any changes had occurred in the previous five centuries. Fourth, chapter 93 of the *Kebre Negast*, an epic account of the founding of the Ethiopian royal dynasty first written down near the end of the Zagwe dynasty in A.D. 1270, includes a strong attack against Nestorianism. Nestorianism was never a threat in Ethiopia; attacks against it could only be sparked by the especially vicious hatred of it held by non-Chalcedonians.

A further proof of the Ethiopians' continued rejection of Chalcedon comes from the mid-thirteen century. During the reign of Emperor Emnet, a dispute broke out within the church as to whether one Sabbath (Sunday) or two Sabbaths (Saturday and Sunday) should be observed. The emperor listened to both sides of the debate and decided for the one Sabbath position, whereupon the two Sabbath supporters accused him of being a supporter "of Pope Leo." Hostility to the pope of Chalcedon was so strongly fixed in the mind of the Ethiopian clergy that they automatically associated him with any position they saw as heretical (Sergew 1972, 284).

From the time Christianity was first established in Ethiopia, then, the Church strongly supported the non-Chalcedonian understanding of the nature of Christ. This position was maintained through an era when the church struggled through external and internal challenges.

Ethiopian Orthodoxy Interacts with the West

The fifteenth century began a period of two hundred years of interaction between the Ethiopian Orthodox Church and Western Christianity, particularly as represented by the Jesuits. This interaction grew out of the context of the strong non-Chalcedonian Christology which was established in Ethiopia and it has established the framework for the Ethiopian church's current understanding of the nature of Christ.

## Initial Contacts

The West's initial interest in Ethiopia Christianity was sparked by the Council of Florence in 1441. The Council was convened at least partially in an attempt to bring unity to the Eastern and Western Churches so that the Eastern Emperor could secure Western aid against the Turks, who were about to attack Constantinople. It appears that Ethiopia was represented at the Council by monks appointed by the superior of the Ethiopian congregation in Jerusalem, Nicodemus, but it is uncertain as to whether these were official representatives of the Ethiopian emperor, Zara Yacob, and the EOC.[10] The

---

[10] Brake discusses in detail whether or not Ethiopian representatives were present at the Council and whether or not they were there in an official or unofficial capacity. His conclusion that the "monks representing the Jerusalem monastery were local representatives and had no official

Council achieved a brief, illusionary unity of the churches which did not last beyond the collapse of Constantinople. The Ethiopian representatives never returned to Ethiopia, and were probably killed in Egypt on their way home (Brake 1972, 113). The only record of the whole affair in Ethiopia is of a certain "Frank" who appeared in the Ethiopian court teaching Roman Christianity, but who was "confounded" by the Ethiopian theologians (Jones and Monroe 1935, 58). Probably the Ethiopians rejected what the monks had done and this record of encounter was the result. Besides demonstrating the Ethiopians' continued rejection of the Council of Chalcedon, the significance of the Council of Florence is that it raised an awareness of Ethiopian Christianity in Europe.

During the reign of Baeda Maryam (1468-78) a form of Eutychianism was introduced into Ethiopia by Syrian and Egyptian monks (Brake 1972, 113-14; Tesfazghi 1973, 55). It is possible that this revival of Eutychianism was an area-wide reaction to the Council of Florence. These monks claimed that Jesus was human, but did not have a human body with real flesh and blood. The debates shows the strength of non-Chalcedonian theology in the EOC at this time and also demonstrates a tendency of some in the Ethiopian church to move toward a more extreme monophysitism which minimizes Christ's humanity.

---

authority to speak for the entire Ethiopian Church" is supported by Tadesse and Geddes (Brake 1972, 112; Tadesse 1972, 265; Geddes 1696, 27-29).

## Portuguese Soldiers and Jesuit Missionaries

Ever since the twelfth century Europeans had been hearing rumors about a wealthy and powerful Christian king named "Prestor John" who lived beyond the Islamic world and who could prove a valuable ally in defeating the Muslims. In the late fifteenth century, when Portugal was exploring Africa and seeking a passage to India, the king of Portugal sent Petro de Covilham to attempt to make contact with this Prestor John. When he arrived at Aden, de Covilham heard of a powerful Christian king in the interior of the horn of Africa, and, after a round trip to India, arrived in the Ethiopian court in 1490. He was never allowed to leave Ethiopia, but his presence influenced the regent queen Helena to write to the king of Portugal in 1507 for aid in the Ethiopians' wars against the Muslims (Hyatt 1928, 33-34).[11]

## Lebna Dengal and the First Portuguese Embassy

An embassy from Portugal arrived in 1520 when Lebna Dengal (1508-40) was king, the first major encounter between Ethiopia and a Western power. The Ethiopians saw the meeting as a chance to form a military alliance against the Muslims attacking Ethiopia and to recruit craftsmen who could help them develop their country. However, the goal of the Portuguese seems to have been to gain Ethiopian support in

---

[11]Geddes says that the new king, Nahod, considered de Covilham to be a spy (Geddes 1696, 41).

case Portugal became involved in a war against Egypt and to gain the submission of the Ethiopian church to the Roman Catholic Church (Yeshaq 1989, 47-49; Jones and Monroe 1935, 78-79).

There is some evidence that Lebna Dengal took a step toward the Catholic faith at this time. In a letter he wrote to the Pope, he says that "all should yield obedience to you . . . . You are my Father and I am your Son," and he asks the Pope to send a "Nuncio" to Ethiopia (Geddes 1696, 65-66). However, Yeshaq says that, though Lebna Dengal was interested in the Catholic Church, he never formally submitted to the Pope (Yeshaq 1989, 48-49). Blyth contends that Lebna Dengal really believed that the Ethiopian Orthodox Church and the Roman Church were essentially one in doctrine (Blyth 1935, 85). Jones and Monroe believe that Lebna Dengal only acknowledged that the Pope was the first bishop of Christendom, but that he never accepted any of the theology of the Roman church (Jones and Monroe 1935, 88). They also point out that the chaplain of the Portuguese embassy, Francisco Alvarez, was no theologian or historian of the early church, and it is probable that neither the Portuguese or the Ethiopians "realized the doctrinal chasm which separated them and the question of the natures of Christ was never raised" (Jones and Monroe 1935, 77). Whatever the case, this first encounter ended with Lebna Dengal sending a letter requesting craftsmen to be sent from Portugal to Ethiopia, but with no formal agreement of cooperation between the Ethiopians and the Portuguese. The Portuguese mission returned to Europe.

Mohammed Gragn

However, six years later, Ethiopia suffered what many historians regard as the worst disaster in its history. Ahmed ibn Ibrahim el Ghazi, known as Mohammed Gragn ("the left handed"), the emir of Harrar invaded highland Ethiopia with the support of Turkish weapons and soldiers, and began devastating the country. Gragn made the church a special target of his attacks, killing priests, destroying churches, and burning manuscripts (Tadesse 1972, 301). Unable to defeat Gragn, Lebna Dengal again sought the aid of the Portuguese. He commissioned a European named Christopher Lecanare (known as Zaga Zabo by the Ethiopians) as ambassador to Ethiopia. Zabo was authorized to write a confession of faith to show that the Ethiopians essentially agreed with Western Christianity in order to solicit military aid from Portugal (Brake 1975, 117-18).

Zabo's confession is significant because, though he stressed the similarity of the Ethiopian church with the West, he clearly articulated a non-Chalcedonian view on the nature of Christ. Zabo affirmed that Jesus was perfect God and perfect man and rejected both Eutychianism and Nestorianism, but he also spoke of Christ as "being perfect God and perfect Man; and having only one aspect," implying the union of Christ's divinity and humanity into a single nature. He went on to say that "the Divinity itself was with his Soul, as it was also with his most holy Body," almost implying the Eutychian position that Christ's divinity absorbed his humanity (Geddes 1696, 82-83; Brake 1975, 119-129). Zabo concludes by promising that the Ethiopian Orthodox Church would submit to "the Roman Pontiff . . . as the Vicar of Christ" (Geddes 1696, 109). Brake says that, in his confession, Zabo was probably trying to "conceal the real differences between the two positions" while "not denying the traditional monophysite doctrine of the church" (Brake 1975, 122). Lebna Dengal also sent a Portuguese resident of Ethiopia, John Bermudez, to encourage Lisbon to support the Ethiopian cause.

Lebna Dengal died in 1540, his country devastated by the invading Muslims. But his efforts bore fruit. Zabo's confession sparked renewed interest in Ethiopia in the Portuguese court, and in 1541 Christopher de Gama arrived in Ethiopia with 400 soldiers. In his initial battle with the Muslims, de Gama was killed. However his troops rallied and, joined by the army of the new Ethiopian emperor, Galawedewos, defeated the Muslim army and killed Gragn (Jones and Monroe 1935, 83-85).

The First Jesuit Mission

The victory over the Muslims, however, marked the beginning of conflict between the Catholics and the Ethiopian Orthodox Church. John Bermudez, who had returned with the

Portuguese, claimed that the dying archbishop of Ethiopia had appointed him as the next archbishop.[12] The remaining Portuguese troops now supported Bermudez's claim. It may be that Galawedewos had actually feigned submission to Bermudez during the Muslim threat in order to be sure of Portuguese support (Brake 1975, 125-26). Now, however, he rejected Bermudez and exiled him (Hyatt 1928, 1935; Yeshaq 1989, 51). The Portuguese reports to Lisbon at this time affirmed the Ethiopian church's clear rejection of Chalcedon, but expressed confidence that Ethiopia could be persuaded to become Catholic. The Pope and the King of Portugal responded by sending Andre Oviedo and an entire mission of Jesuits to minister in Ethiopia (Brake 1975, 127-30)

Oviedo was well received by Galawedewos, who recognized that the Jesuits' skills in theological debate made them formidable opponents for his own clergy (Brake 1975, 130).[13] So he agreed to hold a public debate in which he himself would represent the Ethiopian Orthodox Church. Not

---

[12] Geddes believes Bermudez's claim that Lebna Dengal appointed him to be the Abuna (Geddes 1696, 146). However, Jones and Monroe list a number of reasons why Bermudez' claim was almost certainly fabricated: it is highly unlikely that Lebna Dengal would have suddenly violated centuries of custom in asking a Portuguese Catholic to become Abuna, there is no record of such an appointment either in Rome or in correspondence between Lebna Dengal and Bermudez, and while Bermudez was still alive the Pope appointed another patriarch of Ethiopia (Jones and Monroe 1935, 86).

[13] Geddes quotes one of the Jesuits who says the Ethiopians were particularly hostile to the Council of Chalcedon and Pope Leo (Geddes 1696, 164).

surprisingly, Galawedewos was declared the winner of the debate; more importantly the formal confession he prepared for the debate has endured and presents a clear picture of the Ethiopian Orthodox Church's doctrine at this time (Budge 1928, 353-56; Geddes 1696, 185-89). In it, the emperor identified the Ethiopian Orthodox Church with the ancient councils at Nicea, Constantinople, and Ephesus, "in effect saying he was not a Nestorian or an Eutychian" (Brake 1975, 131), but also pointedly omitting the Council of Chalcedon (Tesfazghi 1973, 58).[14]

Ethiopian reports of this debate claim that the Jesuits emphasized that Jesus had two natures and that the Jesuits used John 14:28 to claim that Jesus was "less than" the Father.[15] The impression of the Ethiopians was that the Catholics believed that Jesus had "two parts" and that one part was something less than God (Tesfazghi 1972, 50-53). Though the Jesuits almost certainly did not teach that Jesus was inferior to the Father, the record of the debates passed down by the Ethiopians reveals their perception of and their intense opposition to Chalcedonian Christology. They would reject any theology that seemed to divide the person of Christ

---

[14] Galawedewos' confession also explains at length that the Jewish practices in the EOC (avoiding pork, Sabbath worship, circumcision) were voluntary customs and not religiously prescribed.

[15] "If you loved me, you would be glad that I am going to the Father, because the Father is greater than I" (NIV). All subsequent references to Scripture will be from the New International Version (NIV) unless otherwise noted.

or make him less than the Father. Though they did not accept the Jesuits' teaching, the Ethiopians allowed them to remain in the country and to carry out a limited ministry.[16]

Galawedewos died in battle in 1559 and his brother, Admas, took the throne. He was more hostile to the Jesuits than his relatively tolerant brother had been; he canceled the Portuguese land grants and, at one point, drew his sword and threatened to kill Oviedo (Ludolphus 1682, 324)! The Jesuits were allowed to remain, but accomplished little. Oviedo died in 1577, and most of the Jesuits died in Ethiopia with few converts.

The Second Jesuit Mission

Rome continued to show interest in Ethiopia and continued to try to get missionaries into the country. All were killed or captured by Muslims as they approached Ethiopia. In 1603, however, Rome was able to ransom Pero Paez from a Muslim prison and he traveled to Ethiopia. Hyatt calls Paez a man of "prudence and ability" (1928, 38) and, instead of engaging in high level debates with kings and priests, he quietly settled in Maiguagua where he established a school and worked as a mason and architect. News of his school traveled to the king, Za Dengal, who invited Paez to the court. Paez came with a number of the children he had been teaching.

---

[16]Oviedo subsequently issued a document listing the errors of the EOC, giving special prominence to the church's teaching that there was "but one Nature, and one Operation in Christ" (Geddes 1696, 198).

Ludolphus reports that the king was impressed with two things. First, Paez had learned Ge'ez and spoke it as well as the Ethiopians themselves. Second, not only did he know his theology, but even the children he had taught could confound the Ethiopian Orthodox Church theologians in debate about the nature of Christ (1682, 326)

Za Dengal proclaimed his intention to convert to Catholicism, but there was an immediate rebellion and he was killed. Under his successor, Suseneyos (1607-32), Paez continued his quiet influence. While Suseneyos consolidated his rule, open debates on the nature of Christ were held, and his brother Ras Sel Chrestos and others converted to Catholicism. The holiness and knowledge of the new converts impressed Suseneyos and others, and the king issued an edict declaring his belief in the two natures of Christ. The Abuna then threatened the king with excommunication. Suseneyos responded by exposing the immoral behavior of the Abuna, ordering the entire kingdom to accept the Chalcedonian formula of the two natures of Christ, and writing Rome to send more Jesuit missionaries (Brake 1975, 135-36; Jones and Monroe 1935, 94-96; Yeshaq 1989, 54).

Throughout the conflict, the central issue remained the nature of Christ (Ludolphus 1682, 329; Yeshaq 1989, 54), revealing that "the doctrine of the one nature of Christ was the all-important doctrine to the Ethiopian Orthodox Church," "the one doctrine that made a person either orthodox or non-orthodox" (Brake 1975, 137). For the Catholics, the key error of the Ethiopian church was their rejection of Chalcedon. In one of his letters to the pope, Ras Sel Chrestos pled for more missionaries to counter "the corrupt doctrine" and "the crooked Faith of Dioscorus" and to bring the Ethiopian church "into the secure harbor of the true faith of St. Leo, the pope of Rome" (Brake 1975, 140). The key theological difference that separated the Jesuits and the EOC was clearly their understanding of the nature of Christ.

In 1622 Paez died, and "overbearing, bigoted" Alphonzo Mendez became head of the Catholic mission (Brake 1975, 139; Ludolphus 1682, 336). Mendez switched from Paez's quiet approach and demanded rebaptism of all Ethiopian Christians into the Catholic church, reconsecration of all Ethiopian churches, re-ordination of all Ethiopian priests, the use of the Roman calendar, and the use Latin in all Ethiopian church services. Ephraim notes that

> the goal of the Catholics was to implant a doctrinal point; that of the Chalcedonian formula of the double nature of Christ. In order to accomplish this, they thought they had to uproot ancient Ethiopian practices such as those pertaining to food regulations, marriage customs and keeping Saturday as Sabbath. (Ephraim 1971, 275)

Suseneyos formally converted to Catholicism and submitted to the pope, but the attacks on ancient customs and liturgy, with the implications that the faith of their fathers was illegitimate, was too much for the country as a whole. There was a "genuine popular insurrection" (Brake 1975, 139) throughout the land and Suseneyos began a bitter civil war to preserve the Catholic faith. After one battle, he and his son, Fasilades, surveyed the carnage, and Fasilades remarked, "This is not a victory over Muslims or heathens, but over our own flesh and blood, our fellow-subjects, our fellow Christians" (Blyth 1935, 87). Shaken, Suseneyos issued an edict in 1632 granting freedom to return to the traditional non-Chalcedonian faith. He then abdicated and died later the same year (Jones and Monroe 1935, 96-98; Yeshaq 1989, 55-56).

Soon after Fasilades (1632-67) took the throne, a debate was held between Alphonzo Mendez and an Ethiopian Orthodox theologian named Betre Giorgis. The central issue of the debate was the two natures of Christ. Betre Giorgis was declared the winner of the debate, and a popular poem was composed by the Ethiopians: "Now we have a rod that will weaken Alphonzo"[17] (Mekarios and others 1996, 138). Fasilades then banished the Catholic missionaries with the words, "the flock of Ethiopia has escaped from the hyenas of the West" (Brake 1975, 153). When he ordered Mendez to leave the country, the new king told him that the Ethiopians had "believed from the beginning" what the Catholic church called the two natures of Christ, his divinity and humanity. "We believe the Lord Christ is perfect God and perfect Man. His natures are not separated nor divided, for neither of them subsist of itself" (Ludolphus 1682, 363-64).

---

[17]"Betre" means "rod" in Ge'ez.

The Jesuits had insisted that the Orthodox adopt Chalcedonian theology as an essential Christian doctrine. The Jesuits' presence, however, had convinced the Ethiopian Orthodox that Chalcedon was both unnecessarily divisive and destructive of their traditional faith. Two hundred years of contact with Western Christians had left the Ethiopian Orthodox Church bitterly hostile toward Chalcedonian theology, convinced that only non-Chalcedonian Christology could be authentically Ethiopian.

## Aftermath

In succeeding years the Ethiopian Orthodox Church was particularly hostile to Chalcedonian Christianity in general and to Catholics in particular. Capuchin missionaries trying to enter Ethiopia in the late seventeenth century were killed. The "Story of the Four Councils" was also written in the seventeenth century. It emphasized that "attributing actions to either the human or divine nature is dividing the person of Christ . . . . Everything he did whether miracle or suffering stemmed from the one God-man nature." The "Story" explained that Jesus had said that the Father was greater than him only out of humility, even as he humbled himself and became lower than the angels and humbled himself to wash the disciples' feet (Brake 1975, 150).

In the eighteenth century, when explorer James Bruce visited Ethiopia, one of the first questions he was asked was whether he believed Christ had two natures or one, demonstrating the intense feelings the Ethiopian Orthodox Church continued to have about this doctrine and their mistrust of what Westerners believed (Jones and Monroe 1935, 124). When Samuel Gobat of the Church Missionary Society came to Ethiopia in the nineteenth century, during his first conversation with the Echegé[18] he was asked what he believed about what the Catholic church called the two natures of Christ. He responded with a question: Did the Echegé believe that Jesus Christ was perfect God and perfect man? When the Echegé answered, "Yes, with all my heart," Gobat responded, "Well we are brothers in this respect, although we express ourselves differently" (Crummey 1972, 32). Gobat's response gained him the opportunity to remain in the capital city of Gondor distributing Scriptures and sharing his faith with everyone who visited him. He concluded that an attack on non-Chalcedonian Christology was an attack on the heart of the Ethiopian Orthodox Church (Brake 1975, 179-80).

The Jesuit mission of the sixteenth and seventeenth centuries is still viewed by Ethiopian Orthodox scholars as destructive to their church and one of the worst examples of Christianity the country has ever experienced. Yeshaq, a modern Ethiopian Orthodox historian, reflects the opinion of many Ethiopian Orthodox.

---

[18]The Echegé was the chief abbot of the monastic house of Tekle Haimanot at Debra Lebanos. Because the Patriarch of the EOC was an Egyptian appointed in Alexandria, the Echegé was the highest ranking Ethiopian national in the church until Basilios became archbishop in 1951.

> The attitude of the Jesuits who were called Christian fathers is a very ugly subject to deal with, although it is something that must be told to generations following. Sometimes it is very difficult to understand whether these Jesuits were Christians or anti-Christians. Apparently, they did not come to Ethiopia with the Gospel of Christ to preach peace and love among people. Instead, they came on political missions carrying with them not the Almighty God, but almighty swords and guns that caused the deaths of hundreds of thousands of Ethiopians . . . . The popes of Rome and the Portugal [sic] kings . . . forced themselves in vain effort [sic] to convert Christians to Christianity. (Yeshaq 1989, 57)

Tadesse, a secular Ethiopian historian, echoes the same thoughts.

> The Jesuit experience was very bitter for the Ethiopian Church . . . . During their short sojourn in Ethiopia, the Jesuits had done a great deal of damage and they had seriously disturbed the spiritual stability of the Ethiopian Church. (Tadesse 1970, 29).

Official publications of the Ethiopian Orthodox Church praise the zealous defense of the true faith by those clergy who stood against Suseneyos and call the work of the Jesuits a "foreign invasion" (Mekarios and others 1996, 137; 139).

The Jesuits' uncompromising stand for Chalcedon was only one reason they were so thoroughly rejected by the Ethiopian Orthodox. Nevertheless, it was an integral part of an experience which is deeply resented by the Orthodox. For many Ethiopian Christians, Chalcedonian theology will always be associated with one of the most destructive attacks on authentic Ethiopian Christianity in their country's history.[19]

---

[19]Ethiopian Catholic theologians who insist that the EOC is non-Chalcedonian only in terminology (and so no substantive issue precludes the church's union with Rome) do not seem to grasp the extent to which "one nature," non-Chalcedonian Christology has become a symbol of Christianity

## Orthodoxy's Internal Debates Over the Nature of Christ

The expulsion of the Jesuits marked the end of the era of direct conflict between Chalcedonian and non-Chalcedonian theologies in Ethiopia. The results of these two hundred years were extreme suspicion of Western Christianity and a renewed interest in doctrinal discussion. Prior to this time, the Ethiopian Orthodox Church had largely affirmed its doctrines because they were passed down as traditions. However, the EOC's theologians had been deeply disturbed by the Jesuits and so felt "the need to re-examine the doctrinal positions of the Church and to purify the Church from possible external influences still lingering even after the expulsion of the missionaries" (Tadesse 1970, 29). The "time of independent thinking" (Brake 1975, 170) which followed led to a serious internal debate which reconfirmed the EOC's commitment to non-Chalcedonian theology.[20]

### Union and Unction

The center of the debate concerned the anointing of Christ. Biblical texts (Luke 4:16; Acts 4:27; 10:38) and the very name "Christ" ("Messiah," "Anointed One") teach that in some sense Jesus was anointed. "Anointing" in the Bible

---

which is truly Ethiopian. History has shaped the present context; current Christological theologizing cannot ignore it.

[20] The development of various doctrinal positions on the anointing of Christ during this period is summarized in Appendix A, and the key positions are succinctly defined in the Glossary of Amharic Terms.

generally refers to a person's appointment to a ministerial office and his receiving power and authority to function in that office. Chalcedonian theology has generally understood that Christ only needed appointment, power, and authority for ministry *in his humanity* (Tesfazghi 1973, 73; Ayala 1981, 93). But the Ethiopian Orthodox Church had placed the single nature of Christ at the center of its teaching. Therefore the question arose among Ethiopian Orthodox Church theologians, "In what sense was Christ anointed?"

Soon after the Jesuits were expelled, two different positions emerged on Christ's anointing. The *Tewahedo* (Union) position was accepted by the monks of the order of Tekle Haimanot in Debra Lebanos; it stated that Christ was anointed before birth when his two natures fused into one nature. The anointing restored to Christ's humanity what was lost in Adam's fall (Jones and Monroe 1935, 110; Ayala 1981, 104). However, to some Ethiopian theologians this seemed to overly divide Christ into two natures, and so resembled the Jesuit/Chalcedonian position. Their alternative was the *Qebat* (Unction) position, accepted by the monks of the order of Ewostatewos, primarily from Gojjam. They believed that "the unction affected the union of both natures" (Brake 1975, 155; Ayala 1981, 104), and they seem to have taught that Jesus' divine nature absorbed his human nature, a Eutychian understanding of the nature of Christ (Brake 1975, 155; Jones and Monroe 1935, 110; Tesfazghi 1973, 80-81, 96).

The *Qebat* gave special attention to Acts 10:38 and emphasized that "the Father is the anointer, the son, the anointed, the Holy Spirit the anointing oil." However, the *Tewahedo* were afraid that this

> produced a degree of subordination in the persons of the Holy Trinity, and, moreover, tended to open the way for a continuing distinction between the Divine and Human natures of Christ . . . . There was no need, the Unionists argued, for separate action by the Holy Spirit; the Son Himself, co-eternal with the Father, had by His act of uniting Divine and human natures ennobled the flesh received from the Blessed Virgin. Their slogan was: "The Son Himself the Anointer; the Son Himself Anointed; the Son Himself the Ointment." (Crummey 1972, 21)[21]

The *Tewahedo* took the slogan, "By union He was made consubstantial with the Father," emphasizing that in the unity of the two natures Christ was fully divine. The *Qebat* countered with the slogan, "Through unction Christ was Son consubstantial with the Father," emphasizing that it was the anointing of Christ which effected the union of his natures, and implying a co-mingling of his divinity and humanity (Hyatt 1928, 102). Both groups argued their positions out of a concern to maintain the single, divine-human nature of Christ.

---

[21] Ayala understands the positions to be reversed: that the Debra Lebanos order claimed that Christ was anointed by the Holy Spirit and the Gojjam order claimed that Christ was himself anointer, anointed, and oil of anointing (Ayala 1981, 91-109). However, Ayala understands there to be only two positions, not three (see below pages 82-84 and footnote 25) and is seeking to present the Debra Lebanos position as nearly identical to Chalcedon. Jowett's (1824) first-hand account of the positions in the early nineteenth century makes it clear that the Tewahedo believed that Christ himself was anointer, anointed, and oil of anointing.

It is difficult today to determine the exact position of both groups because each misrepresented the other and each used the key words of their opponent ("union" and "unction") to define their own position (Tesfazghi 1973, 74-77). Recent official publications of the Ethiopian Orthodox Church[22] brand the *Qebat* as adoptionistic[23] (Aymro and Joachim 1979, 132-133; Habte 1964-65, 155). However a more careful study of what the groups actually teach, particularly in Tesfazghi (1973) and Brake (1975), demonstrates that labeling *Qebat* as adoptionistic is, at best, simplistic and, at worst, a misrepresentation of their position.[24]

Through the reigns of six emperors *Tewahedo* and *Qebat* battled for supremacy. Synods and debates were held, wars were fought, murders committed, coups arranged, and excommunications pronounced. Some emperors supported *Tewahedo*, others *Qebat*. In 1687 Emperor Eyasu I sent monks of both orders to a monastery on an island in Lake Tana to discuss the issue, but no solution could be agreed upon (Brake 1975, 160). During the reign of Dawit (1716-21) the Patriarch of Alexandria was asked to formulate a compromise. Abuna Krestodulos suggested a new creed to unite both factions: "By

---

[22] *Tewahedo* is now the official position of the EOC.

[23] Adoptionism refers to the belief that Jesus was only a man whom God the Father "adopted" and made divine in order to carry out his mission.

[24] Tesfazghi specifically says that Aymro and Joachim are "not accurate" in their presentation of *Qebat* and the Three Births position (Tesfazghi 1975, 82).

Union the Son is only begotten Son and by Unction He became Christ." But this was seen as supporting the *Tewahedo* and so was rejected by the *Qebat*, sparking new conflict (Brake 1975, 163; Hyatt 1928, 103).

## Son of Grace, Three Births and the "Knife"

During the reign of Eyasu II (1730-55) a third position called *Yetsegga Leg* ("Son of Grace") emerged.[25] "*Yetsegga Leg* maintains that Christ was not co-eternal with the Father but was adopted Son of God by grace at his baptism" (Aren 1978, 77). *Yetsegga Leg* was soon extended into an even more radical doctrine, however, called *Sost Ledet* ("Three Births").

> Christ, it was argued, was thrice born: once from the Father from all time; once in the Incarnation in the womb of the Blessed Virgin; once through the subsequent action of the Holy Spirit (either still in the womb, or, yet more radically, in the River Jordan; opinion was divided). Here the tendency towards Adoptionism was clear. (Crummey 1972, 24-25)[26]

---

[25] The origins of *Yetsegga Leg* may go back to the time of the Jesuit presence in Ethiopia, but the group did not become prominent until the mid-eighteenth century (Aren 1978, 77). However, Ayala strongly contends that there are only two theological positions: *Tewahedo/Karra* and *Qebat/Sost Ledet/Tsegga Leg* (Ayala 1981, 109-17). He lists six scholars who support the idea of there being only two groups, but mentions twelve scholars who understand there to be three groups. Almost all sources, including a letter from the patriarch of Alexandria in the early nineteenth century, agree with the position taken here that at least three distinct groups emerged (Jowett 1824, 181-94).

[26] Ayala argues that the *Tsegga Leg/Sost Ledet* position was not adoptionistic, since it was understood that only the human nature of Christ was affected by this third birth, and only the human nature which was "Son by Grace" (Ayala 1981, 105-7). Ayala's argument supports his understanding of the

The *Yetsegga Leg* or *Sost Ledet* soon "won over the last institutional basis of *Tewahedo*—the Debra Libanos clergy" (Crummey 1972, 23),[27] but opposition continued from the *Qebat* and from a small number of *Tewahedo* adherents in northern Ethiopia, now given the derogatory name of *Karra* ("Knife")[28] because they "cut off" the third birth of Christ by the Holy Spirit (Crummey 1972, 26).

By the nineteenth century the debate had become a part of the political conflict which divided Ethiopia; each theological position was supported by a different region of the country. As part of their attempt to unify Ethiopia, Emperor Yohannis and his designated heir, Menelik, convened an

---

*Tsegga Leg* position as being essentially Chalcedonian.

[27] One reason why Ayala may combine the *Sost Ledet* and *Tewahedo* positions is because *Sost Ledet* became the predominate opinion among the monks at Debra Lebanos who had formerly been the strongest advocates of the *Tewahedo*.

[28] There is a great deal of confusion in the literature regarding names. Because both the *Qebat* and the *Tewahedo* opposed the *Sost Ledet*, some writers are unclear as to which of them was actually identified as *Karra*. Some do not distinguish them as separate positions (Ayala 1981; c.f. Brake 1975, 188-89); others see *Karra* as a fourth position, distinct from both *Qebat* and *Tewahedo* (Brake 1975, 260). Hyatt and Yeshaq associate the *Karra* position with the Eustathians (who were traditionally *Qebat*) and Yeshaq calls *Karra* "Wold Qib," the position associated with the *Qebat* (Hyatt 1928, 104; Yeshaq 1989, 66). But Yeshaq also distinguishes the *Qebat* from the *Karra/Wold Qib*! Because both *Qebat* and *Karra* held to Christ's "two births" and opposed *Sost Ledet* they are often confused. The majority of writers simply understand the *Karra* as another name for the *Tewahedo* position (Aren, 1978, 78; Crummey 1972, 24; Tesfazghi 1973, 74-82; c.f. Jowett 1824, 181-94; see sources listed in Ayala 1981, 109-17). See Appendix A for a chart summarizing the development of the positions.

assembly at Boru Meda in 1878 to eliminate the dispute. Assisted by a letter from Abba Qerlos, the patriarch of Egypt, the council condemned the *Sost Ledet* and affirmed the *Tewahedo* or *Karra* position. Christ was said to be God by nature, born eternally of the Father and of Mary as a human; he himself was the unction by which he was anointed (Zewdu 1991, 48; Tesfazghi 1973, 84-86). "Three Birth" supporters who protested the decision had their tongues cut out (Hyatt 1928, 104). When Yohannis died, Menelik II assumed the throne, and though he never called a Council, he promoted the *Tewahedo* position, and "*de facto* it has reigned peacefully" as the official position of the Ethiopian Orthodox Church ever since (Tesfazghi 1973, 86).

## Significance of the Debate on Christ's Anointing

Non-Ethiopian theologians may find it difficult to understand why so much energy was expended and so much blood was spilled over the debate on Christ's anointing. The importance of the debate, however, is clear when one sees it in the light of the EOC's strong non-Chalcedonian Christology. "The purpose of the subtle argument on unction in Ethiopian Christology is to demonstrate whether one accepts a duality of natures in Christ or not" (Tesfazghi 1973, 88). Ethiopian Orthodox theologians wanted to "ward off the ever present danger of the Catholic doctrine of the two natures of Christ" (Hyatt 1928, 102). The debates grew out of this concern and their intensity demonstrates how much the Ethiopian Orthodox wanted to avoid any association with Chalcedon.

But the resolution of the dispute on Christ's anointing at Boru Meda also has significance for understanding the EOC's perspective on Christ's nature. On the one hand, the condemnation of the *Sost Ledet* demonstrates the EOC's intense opposition to any theological position which seems to promote two natures in Christ or which seems to elevate the humanity of Christ at the expense of his deity, the ultimate concerns of the EOC's non-Chalcedonian Christology. On the other hand, the triumph of *Tewahedo* over *Qebat* demonstrates the EOC's commitment to maintaining the genuine humanity of Christ, unmixed with his deity, and to avoid slipping into Eutychianism. The Council of Boru Meda laid the foundation for the EOC's present position of affirming Christ's perfect deity and perfect humanity in one nature.

## Formal Perspectives on the Nature of Christ in the Ethiopian Orthodox Church

The position of the Ethiopian Orthodox Church today on the nature of Christ is the result of its birth as a non-Chalcedonian church, its conflicts with the Jesuits, and its internal struggles to define its position on Christ's anointing. Official publications of the EOC and published works by individual Ethiopian Orthodox theologians affirm both the single nature of Christ and his full deity and humanity.

## Official Publications of the Ethiopian Orthodox Church

Aymro and Joachim (1970) is an official publication of the Ethiopian Orthodox Church which is intended to explain the church's beliefs to the rest of the Christian world. As such, its statement on the nature of Christ is very important, and will be quoted at length.

> Christ is one Incarnate nature of God the Word. After the union it is impossible to speak of Christ as being in two natures. By the union of the natures in the Incarnation the two natures became one nature, the natures being united without separation, without confusion, and without change. Neither of the natures was assimilated by the other, the properties of the Divine Word were attributed to the flesh and those of the flesh to the Divine Word. The Logos revealed Himself in our flesh and became man like us. He did all things that man does with the exception of sin (John 8:46). And at the same time he was truly God. He is God-Man. He is co-equal and consubstantial with the Father in his Godhead. He is perfectly united with us; the union being from two modes of life into one. The union of the Word with the flesh took place in the womb of the Virgin Mary. St. John says: "The Word was made flesh . . . ." In the same way we can say that also the flesh was made divine. The attributes of the flesh can be given to the Divine Word and vice versa. However, the properties of each nature are preserved without change after the union . . . . We hold "mia physis", composite nature, one united nature. Again the Lord Jesus Christ is perfect man and perfect God . . . . We accept both unity and duality in Christ who in acting performed as one. Christ, in whom humanity and divinity were united in one Person and one Nature, was crucified on the cross . . . . If . . . only the human body was crucified, He could not save the world. (Aymro and Joachim 1970, 95-96)

The statement goes on to accept the teachings of Cyril and Dioscorus, but to reject Eutyches and the idea that Christ's divine nature absorbed or overshadowed his human nature. Aymro and Joachim specifically deny that Christ is two persons or two natures, "but being at once divine and human."

Several observations may be made from this statement of faith. First, the Ethiopian Orthodox Church strongly emphasizes the unity of Christ. Though he was out of two natures, the two were united into one nature in the womb of the Virgin Mary. "Two modes of life" were united into one. Christ is one "composite nature, one united nature" who always acts as a single, unified person. In particular, his crucifixion was not merely in his humanity, but was in his united person and nature. To underline the unity of the person of Christ, the EOC speaks of the properties of the Word being attributed to the flesh and those of the flesh to the Divine Word.

Second, though the EOC believes that Christ's two natures were united into a single nature, it officially affirms the full humanity of Christ. He was "perfect God and perfect man." The Church believes that his natures were united "without confusion, without change" and that "the properties of each nature are preserved without change after the union;" that is, Christ's divinity and humanity were not absorbed into one another nor did one destroy the other. The EOC thus officially rejects Eutychian or Apollinarian ideas that the union of the two natures made Christ something less than fully human. The Church affirms that Christ "became man like us" and did everything that humans do but sin.[29]

---

[29]Ethiopian Catholic theologians such as Tesfazghi (1973), Ayala (1981), and Musay (1997) point to the EOC's strong formal affirmation of Christ's full deity and full

Third, though the EOC affirms Christ's full humanity, there are hints that the Church believes his humanity was somehow different from that of other people. Not only did the Word become flesh, but "the flesh was made divine." Though the Church affirms that Christ's humanity and deity were united, "without confusion," it also believes that "the attributes of the flesh can be given to the Divine Word and vice versa." Christ's humanity received the attributes of his deity.[30] Statements such as these seem to reflect Apollinarian and Eutychian ideas that Christ's humanity was touched and changed by his deity.[31]

Finally, this doctrinal statement reveals that one of the main concerns of the Ethiopian Orthodox Church is to prevent overly dividing Christ into two persons, reflecting

---

humanity--especially their use of Chalcedonian terminology such as "without confusion" and "without change"--and conclude that the EOC is Chalcedonian in actual belief, and non-Chalcedonian only in terminology (Ayala 1981, 69-70).

[30] The idea that Christ's humanity is different from that of other human beings is reflected in a popular way EOC theologians describe the incarnation: God became man and *man became God*. The idea is that Christ's humanity was touched and transformed by his deity.

[31] Ayala quotes EOC sources which teach that Christ's divine and human attributes did *not* mingle and that Christ's suffering was "in his flesh" as evidence that the EOC really believes in two natures of Christ (Ayala 1981, 88). However, he overlooks other formal statements from the EOC which imply a mingling of divine and human attributes as well as the EOC's strong emphasis that Christ never acted strictly as a human or strictly as God. The apparent contradictions in formal EOC statements of faith reflect a tension between the church's desire to preserve its non-Chalcedonian heritage and to teach the full deity and humanity of Christ.

monophysitism's historical obsession with the danger of Nestorianism. Everything Christ did, including dying on the cross, he did as a single, unified person.

Christ's full deity and humanity and the unity of his natures is also stressed in other official publications of the church. The Ethiopian Orthodox theologians quoted in Matthews emphasize that "without being separated in substance from the right hand of the Father" the eternal Word

> took in His separate Person from the womb of the Virgin Mary flesh from her flesh, soul from her soul, and Godhead was united with Manhood . . . . 'Christ' is the name of union. (Matthews 1936, 12)

Christ has the same substance as the Father and the same flesh and soul as Mary; he is fully God and fully man. However, the term "Christ" ("anointed") does not refer to his humanity alone, but to his unified person. The two natures were perfectly united into one.

Recent publications of the Ethiopian Orthodox Church also give a very clear statement of the Church's response to Chalcedon. Representatives from the EOC participated in a series of talks held between Chalcedonian and non-Chalcedonian Eastern Orthodox Churches between 1964 and 1993. During the talks themselves the EOC representatives emphasized that they could not be expected to accept the Chalcedonian formula (Third and fourth consultations 1971, 30). At the conclusion of these it was agreed that there was no basic difference in the Christology of the two groups: both groups condemned Nestorius and Eutyches and "those who speak in terms of 'two' do not thereby divide or separate and those who speak in terms of 'one' do not thereby commingle, (mingle) or confuse" (Mekarios and others 1996, 144; see also Papandreou and Bishoy 1990, 9-11). Representatives from both the Chalcedonian and non-Chalcedonian Orthodox Churches agreed that "both families have loyally maintained the authentic Orthodox Christological doctrine" and that each should lift the anathemas pronounced against the other (Papandreou and Bishoy 1993, 17). In spite of this agreement, the EOC's official response to the talks was that

> "Two natures, two wills, two energies hypostatically united in the One Lord Jesus Christ", was not felt to be the same as that of the Oriental Orthodox Churches Christological formula of "one nature, one will and one energy in the one and the same Christ." (Mekarios and others 1996, 145)

The EOC refused to lift the anathemas on the Chalcedonian fathers, continued to emphasize that it accepts no ecumenical council after Ephesus (A.D. 431), and called on the Chalcedonian churches to accept a Christological formula of the unity of the two natures of Christ into one nature (Mekarios and others 1996, 128, 145-46). Even though some EOC leaders occasionally refer to the difference between their theology and Chalcedonian theology as "terminological" (Eadie 1973, 142), Chalcedon continues to be an unacceptable Christological formula for the official hierarchy of the Ethiopian Orthodox Church.

## Other Ethiopian Orthodox Writers

Publications by Ethiopian Orthodox theologians which speak of the nature of Christ strongly affirm the church's official teaching on the nature of Christ. Habte affirms that Christ's two natures are combined into one nature, but anathemizes "those who say that Christ's humanity was absorbed or swallowed up in His Divinity." Christ's single nature is important because he "could not save the world" if he were not "united in one person and one nature" when he was crucified (Habte 1964-65, 158). The EOC speaks of one nature "to condemn the Nestorian heresy of dividing the one Christ into two natures" (Habte 1964-65, 160).

Ethiopian Orthodox writers express particular concern at the Chalcedonian tendency to attribute some of Christ's actions to his divine nature and others to his human nature. Poladian criticizes Pope Leo for assigning Jesus' hunger, thirst, weariness, and sleep to his human nature but his feeding of the five thousand and offering of living water to his divine nature. "At Chalcedon no real union was obtained. The human and divine natures were each left as separate entities, not really united." If only Christ's human nature suffered, "God is still not after all living a human life." He is "still holding himself at a distance from its experiences and conditions" (Poladian 1964, 258-259). Instead

> all concerning Christ should be applied to His entire person as one Lord . . . . God suffered, God was crucified, God shed blood, God died, and God was risen up for the salvation of all men . . . . If God the Word had

not suffered on the Cross, the Christian hope for eternal salvation is vanity. (Yeshaq 1989, 103)

Amharic language writers from the EOC echo these same concerns for attributing certain actions of Christ to his human or divine nature. While agreeing that Jesus was a perfect human being who did not sin, Asarat emphasizes that he had to be one person, one nature and one will in order to provide salvation.

> If we say Christ performed divine acts in his divinity and human acts in his humanity, then salvation is only in his humanity, and the price God paid is useless; a human salvation is insufficient. Perfect union of divinity and deity without destroying either is necessary.[32] (Asarat 1990, 152-53)

Pointing to Colossians 1:22 and 1 Peter 3:18 and 4:1 for support, Asarat emphasizes that "the Divine Son died" (1990, 153), and Berhanu says "God died by means of flesh" (1993, 47). Berhanu criticizes Pope Leo's position as being practically the same as Nestorius. "He claimed [Christ's] divinity performed divine works and his humanity performed human works. This is outside of the teaching of the apostles and the Bible" (Berhanu 1993, 48). If Christ's divinity remains somehow distinct from his humanity, God has not drawn near to man and mankind cannot be saved. Instead, Berhanu affirms that Christ became one nature "without destroying his humanity or deity in order to save. So he was perfect God and perfect man" (Berhanu 1993, 49).

---

[32]All quotes from Asarat and Berhanu are the author's own translation from Amharic.

Tesfazghi lists the responses of six EOC theologians to Ayala's contention that EOC is essentially in agreement with Chalcedon. Five of the six vehemently attack both Ayala's suggestion and Chalcedon. The sixth responds with a more congenial spirit, but, in the end, continues to reject Chalcedon and any Christological formula that speaks of Christ as being "in two natures" (Tesfazghi 1973, 153-67).

Both official publications of the Ethiopian Orthodox Church and writings of Ethiopian Orthodox theologians, then, affirm Christ's full deity and humanity while putting the greatest attention on the unity of those two natures. Unless that unity is expressed as a single person *and* a single nature, EOC theologians feel that the one Christ will become two and Christ's death will not accomplish salvation.

### Linguistic Perspectives on the Nature of Christ in the Ethiopian Orthodox Church

The Ethiopian Orthodox Church's fears of overly dividing Christ are exacerbated by a problem of semantics. The word usually used in Amharic publications of the Ethiopian Orthodox Church to speak of the "nature " of Christ is *baheriy*.[33] However, Tesfazghi gives a lengthy discussion of three words which have been used to speak of the "nature/s" of

---

[33]Seen by comparing the Amharic and English of EOTCHS (1983, 28) and Mekarios (1996, 146). All Amharic words are the author's own transliterations from the Amharic alphabet, and so spellings may vary from quoted sources. See the Glossary of Amharic Terms for a brief definition of all words used for "nature" and "person."

Christ in the writings of Ethiopian Orthodox theologians. All three words--*helawi* ("being, existence"), *baheriy* ("nature, character, essence, personality, trait, attribute, temperament"), and *tebay* ("nature, character, disposition, conduct, temperament,")[34]--are used almost interchangeably. Furthermore, they are all also used to speak of the "person" (Amharic: *akal*) of Christ. Translations from ancient Greek documents use these four terms interchangeably to translate ὑποστασις, φυσις and οὐσια (1973, 23-46). Tesfazghi concludes his careful study of the terms used.

> If we add to '*hellawie*' and '*bahrey*' (and sometimes also to '*tabayee*') the number 'two' (*kel-ettu*), it would signify to the Ethiopian Orthodox theologians 'two persons or two hypostasis or two '*prosopa*' or 'two *natures*' but separately [sic] existing or subsisting in themselves . . . . "*Tabayee*" besides "*bahrey*" (nature) also signifies "*akal*", whether in Christology or in the Holy Trinity. (Tesfazghi 1973, 45)

All of the words which can be used to describe the nature of Christ imply a separate, distinct person of their own. Therefore it is very difficult to describe Christ as two natures in one person. Rather, describing Christ as two natures sounds like Nestorianism to Ethiopian Orthodox Church theologians.

Ayala carefully examines several Amharic and Ge'ez words used to translate φυσις/οὐσια/nature and προσωπον/ὑποστασις/person. He points out that

---

[34] Definitions taken from Leslau (1976, 1; 85; 231). *Baheriy* and *tebay* are treated as virtual synonyms by Leslau, Asarat (1991, 152) and by Tesfazghi and his sources.

> by "nature", the Orthodox Ethiopians also mean the
> spiritual and material components of man, taken
> separately, and for "person", what results from these
> components, in other words, the complete man . . . . The
> word 'nature" is used in so concrete, so realistic a
> sense, that to admit two in Christ repels them and seems
> something monstrous, such as might be felt in saying that
> a person has four legs, or four eyes, and so on . . . . In
> the minds of the Orthodox Ethiopians, the term "*baherey*"
> (=nature), stands for a complete reality that has
> existence by itself, either in an hypostasis or in a
> person. (Ayala 1981, 67; 72)

Because a "nature" is a concrete idea that always results in a "person", to speak of two natures in Christ infers two persons. As a Catholic Ethiopian, Ayala concludes that the terms for "nature" and "person" must be abandoned, and that Christ should be described as "one being, one individual, one single substance, one single subject of attribution; Jesus Christ is a true and perfect man, a true and perfect God" (Ayala 1981, 73).

Tesfazghi's and Ayala's studies are supported by Alemayehu, Berhanu and Kidan. Alemayehu feels that there is not an appropriate translation of φυσις ("nature") in Amharic. *Baheriy* and *tebay* are synonyms which mean nature, "but it doesn't stand there. Nature, character, behavior: so many different meanings." Two natures implies "that Christ has two behaviors." To the average Amharic speaker, speaking of two "natures" implies "two contradictory ways of thinking, two contradictory frames-of-mind, as if Christ could quarrel with himself." The idea of Christ having two natures is offensive to most people; they simply can't understand it (Alemayehu 1995b). Berhanu agrees, saying that "a person (*akal*) without a nature (*baheriy*) or a nature without a person doesn't make sense. If there are two natures, there must be two persons" (Berhanu 1993, 48).

Kidan's Ge'ez-Amharic dictionary further confirms the conclusions of Tesfazghi, Ayala, Berhanu, and Alemayehu. Kidan defines *baheriy* as "the intrinsic elements not fully formed into a nature; the elements by which nature forms its shape."[35] *Baheriy* is the "internal constitutive elements" of a nature. Though *baheriy* is not the same as *akal*, it always acts through *akal*. A *baheriy* always manifests itself through an *akal*: they cannot be separated. As an example, Kidan says one doesn't speak of a sickle cutting grain, but of a person cutting grain, because the sickle is only the instrument; the person is doing the cutting. In the same way that a person expresses himself through the sickle, so the *baheriy* expresses itself through the *akal*. One can never attribute an action to *baheriy*. The ramifications of Kidan's discussion for Christological understanding are clear. One cannot speak of two natures (*baheriy*) and one person (*akal*) because a *baheriy* always has to express itself through an *akal*.

Tesfazghi's summary of the issue of Christological terms is that

> the problem of terminology in our Ethiopian theology . . . will remain as long as the ancient (i.e. pre-Chalcedonian) idioms are still used. In other words, when one disputes about "nature" in the Chalcedonian or Neo-Chalcedonian

---

[35]Translation by author and Musay (1997).

> sense, the Ethiopian thinkers speak of 'person' in the pre-Chalcedonian sense. (1973, 27-28)

It is very difficult to speak of Christ's "two natures" in either Ethiopia's national language or her church language without also implying that Christ himself was divided into two persons.

## Conclusion

Evaluation of popular perspectives on the nature of Christ among Ethiopian Orthodox must take place within the context of how the EOC's understanding of Christ has developed historically, the Church's formal understanding of Christ's nature, and the terms used to talk about Christ's "nature."

Historically, non-Chalcedonian Christology has been one of the identifying marks of indigenous, truly Ethiopian Christianity. The Church was established by those who came to Ethiopia because of their opposition to Chalcedon. Conflicts with Jesuit missionaries in the sixteenth and seventeenth centuries centered around Chalcedonian Christology; rejection of the Jesuits and Chalcedon was identified with preservation of Ethiopia's national identity and authentically Ethiopian Christianity. Hundreds of years of theological debate within the church has centered around the need to defend the church's "one unified nature" understanding Christ. Theologizing on the nature of Christ in modern Ethiopia cannot ignore the way history has conditioned EOC theologians to think of "one-nature" and "two-nature" Christologies.

The historical context has shaped the EOC's present, official stand on the nature of Christ. Shenk has observed that "lacking a widespread 'Reformation' Ethiopian Christianity became a touchstone of national identity without sufficient critique of its essential nature" (Shenk 1988, 278). Shenk's comments seem particularly valid when evaluating the EOC doctrine of the nature of Christ in light of the history of the doctrine's development. Throughout its history, the EOC developed an attachment to certain Christological symbols--loyalty to Alexandria, rejection of both Eutyches and Nestorius, rejection of "Leo" and "Chalcedon," union, one nature--which became synonymous with Christianity that is authentically Ethiopian. The EOC rejects Chalcedon and any "two nature" understanding of Christ for genuine theological reasons--in order to preserve the unity of his person and actions--but also because of a deep historical commitment to a Christology that is identified as Ethiopian.

In addition, discussion of Christ's nature in either Amharic or Ge'ez is complicated because any attempt to distinguish Christ's two natures implies that he was also two persons, perhaps with a mind divided against himself.

Contextual theologians in Ethiopia must recognize the EOC's present theological concerns, the importance of those symbols which have become identified with Ethiopian Christology, and the linguistic factors which shape people's perceptions on the nature of Christ. However, before theologizing, they must also investigate the degree to which all these factors have influenced popular perspectives on the nature of Christ. Historical, formal and linguistic perspectives on the nature of Christ form a framework for understanding and evaluating popular perspectives on the nature of Christ.

# CHAPTER 4
## RESEARCH METHODOLOGY

For centuries the Ethiopian Orthodox Church has been distinguished by its rejection of the Chalcedonian understanding of Christ's two natures combined in one person in favor of the belief that the divine and human natures of Jesus Christ have united into a single nature. The history of the church is marked with a both a deepening commitment to and a progressive clarification of how the church has understood this non-Chalcedonian Christology, and the contemporary church has published clear statements on how it understands the person and nature of Christ. But it is less clear how the nature of Christ is popularly understood among members of the Orthodox church. Evangelicals and other Christians from a Chalcedonian tradition who live in Ethiopia need an understanding of Orthodox perceptions on the nature of Christ in order to avoid misunderstanding and to engage in effective ministry among them. Therefore, a further understanding of popular perspectives on the nature of Christ in the Ethiopian Orthodox Church is needed.

## Operational Questions

In order to begin understanding popular perspectives on the nature of Christ in the EOC, ethnographic interviews were held with fifty-one subjects to explore the research question. As an outworking of the basic research question, operational questions were used to guide the development of specific interview questions.

OQ 1. How do members of the EOC describe Christ's nature?

OQ 2. How do members of the EOC describe Christ's divinity and his humanity?

OQ 3. How do members of the EOC describe the union of Christ's divinity and his humanity?

OQ 4. How do members of the EOC respond to the idea that Christ had two natures?

OQ 5. How do members of the EOC respond to passages in the Bible that imply that Christ sometimes acted completely as a human being, apart from any divine attributes?

OQ 7. How do members of the EOC describe their own relationship with Christ?

## Population

The population for the interviews were individuals who live in the Alert/Gebre Kristos neighborhood in Addis Ababa and who presently identify their religion (Amharic: *haimanot*) as Orthodox Christian. From among this population, at least three different levels of knowledge about religious matters were expected (Teshager 1959, Levine 1965, Imbakom 1970, Ephraim 1971, Seeyoum 1995). Men are usually given more formal religious training than women. Therefore, it was decided to specify men and women as distinct groups among the population to be targeted. Second, men who are members of one of three positions in the Orthodox Church (priest, monk, *debtara*) or who are preparing for one those offices (deacon) receive more religious training than the average male. Therefore, the population was specified to include three distinct groups: laywomen, laymen, and clergy who hold one of these three offices in the Orthodox Church.

## Selection of Subjects

The researcher had lived in Ethiopia for thirteen years when the interviews were conducted, and had sufficient ability in the Amharic language to conduct the interviews. During five of the initial eight interviews a native Amharic speaker who also had an understanding of theological English accompanied the researcher. A second Amharic speaker with an understanding of theological English accompanied the interviewer for nine of the remaining forty-three interviews. The presence of these native Amharic speakers confirmed that adequate comprehension was being obtained by the researcher.

As the limitations of the study did not demand that subjects be selected on the basis of probability sampling, non-probability sampling techniques (Monette, Sullivan, and DeJong 1990, 150-56) were used to obtain subjects for interviews. Subjects were obtained in three ways. First, fourteen interviews were conducted with subjects with whom the researcher had had previous contact. Because the researcher had lived in the Alert/Gebre Kristos neighborhood for thirteen years at the time of the interviews, he knew a large number of people who identified themselves as Orthodox Christians. Of these fourteen, ten interviews were conducted with individuals with whom the researcher had previously held conversations and who were acquaintances of the researcher. With one exception, none of these ten subjects had previously held *theological* conversations with the researcher. Though their acquaintance with the researcher might have predisposed them to give answers agreeable to the researcher in order to "help" him, because the subject was new to their relationship with the researcher, none of them knew what kind of answers would "help" him. In addition, the researcher encouraged these ten subjects that they would provide the greatest assistance to him if they expressed their genuine feelings about each answer. The answers given by these ten subjects did not follow any consistent pattern, providing some indication that they were relatively honest reflections of the subjects' genuine perspectives.

One of the ten subjects with whom the researcher had had previous acquaintance had previously held theological conversations with him. None of these previous conversations, however, had involved a discussion of the nature of Christ.

Though he clearly identified himself as a non-evangelical Ethiopian Orthodox, this subject had previously had extensive conversations with evangelicals other than the researcher. The possibility that his answers were influenced by his knowledge of evangelical theology and his desire to please the researcher was noted in the research notes, and is included in the findings. An additional four interviews were conducted with individuals whom the interviewer had had previous contact, but with whom he had not previously held any extended conversation. Therefore, a total of fourteen subjects were selected based on the interviewer's previous contact with the subjects and knowledge that they identified themselves as Orthodox Christians.

The second way subjects were selected was through contact with a third party. Similar to "snowball sampling" (Monette, Sullivan, DeJong, 1990, 152-53), the fourteen subjects previously known by the researcher were asked to recommend others who would be willing to be interviewed. Twenty-three subjects were selected in this way. Of these twenty-three, thirteen were referred to the researcher on the compound of the Gebre Kristos Church itself by clergy of the church who had been subjects themselves. Other individuals who identified themselves as Orthodox Christians and were previously unknown to the researcher were referred to him by those living in the Alert/Gebre Kristos neighborhood and who were aware of his research interest. Eleven subjects were selected in this way. A total of thirty-four subjects were referred to the researcher by a third-party.

Three subjects were selected randomly. One was a teenager who was a regular attender at the Gebre Kristos, and whom the researcher met on the street. The second was a government administrator in the local *kebele* ("precinct") office whom the researcher met when he inquired about demographic information in the *kebele*. The last subject met at random was a deacon at the Gebre Kristos church. In order to make contact with clergy at the church, the researcher made a visit to the church soon after he began to conduct interviews. In the outer courtyard of the church, he began a conversation with a number of worshippers, telling them he was interested in learning more about the Orthodox Church. One of the worshippers made contact with a deacon of the church who was regarded as one of the primary teachers of the church. The researcher explained to this deacon the purpose of his research and was granted an interview. The deacon subsequently served as the researcher's "intermediary or go-between" (Fetterman 1989, 43) to other clergy at Gebre Kristos.

Throughout the process of selecting subjects, *stratified selection* (Monette, Sullivan, and Dejong 1990, 139) was used to obtain interviews with individuals in all three targeted groups and to contact an equal level of laymen and laywomen. Nineteen laymen and nineteen laywomen were interviewed as subjects. Thirteen members of the clergy were also interviewed as subjects: four priests, four deacons, two monks, two debtara, and one priest who had not yet married and indicated that he might yet become a monk.

Three prospective subjects were interviewed, but were not included as subjects because, during the interviews, it became apparent that they no longer identified themselves as Ethiopian Orthodox believers. Though they initially agreed that their religion was "Orthodox" or "Orthodox Christian," they subsequently said they were no longer Orthodox.

Prior to selecting any subjects, the proposed selection methods were discussed with Dr. Seeyoum Gebre Selassie, Professor of Sociology at Addis Ababa University. Dr. Seeyoum suggested that the researcher introduce himself to potential subjects as a "student of religion" in his own country who was preparing a paper to explain Ethiopian Orthodoxy to his own people. The researcher's teachers required him to talk to a certain number of Ethiopian Orthodox priests and a certain number of ordinary ("*tera*") Orthodox Christians. Because religious teachers tend to be respected in the Ethiopian context, this introduction of the research topic would help potential subjects to feel more comfortable discussing religious matters with a foreign researcher (Seeyoum 1995). Dr. Seeyoum's suggestions were followed by the researcher and proved very effective in opening doors for interviews.

## Instrument

The instrument used to conduct the research was an interview protocol developed based on the issues concerning the nature of Christ that have emerged through the history of the debate and the present official statements of the Orthodox Church as defined in the Operational Questions. Before use, the instrument was also discussed with Dr. Seeyoum Gebre Selassie. Dr. Seeyoum was asked how to improve the instrument to determine subjects' perspectives on the nature of Christ. He made several suggestions as to how to phrase questions in Amharic to make them clearer. He also suggested a line of questioning about Christ's role as an *amelaj* (intercessor-mediator),[1] which proved very valuable in questioning subjects (Seeyoum 1995). The instrument varied slightly depending on the answers given by each subject, but the basic questions remained standard in every interview.

The interview questions were further refined during the initial eight interviews. During five of these interviews the researcher was accompanied by a native Amharic speaker who was familiar with theological English. His presence assured the researcher that adequate understanding was being achieved, and led to slight modifications in the way some of the questions were phrased in Amharic.

---

[1] See note on page 9 and Glossary of Amharic Terms.

## Interview Questions[2]

Interview Question 1. How do you understand the "nature" (*baheriy* or *tebay*) of Jesus Christ?

Interview Question 2. How do you understand Jesus Christ's "being" (*helawi*)? How would you describe his "person" (*akal*)?

Interview Question 3. Was Jesus Christ God, man, or both God and man when he was on earth? How do you understand the way in which his humanity and divinity were joined together?

Interview Question 4. Did Jesus Christ ever hunger, thirst, get tired, or suffer when he was on earth? How could this be possible if he were God?

Interview Question 5. Jesus Christ once told his disciples he didn't know the time of his return to earth? Since God knows everything, if Christ was God, how could he have said this?

Interview Question 6. Now that Jesus Christ has ascended to heaven, is he God, or man or both God and man?

Interview Question 7. If a person said that he believed Christ had two natures--a divine nature and a human nature--how would you respond?

Interview Question 8. Was Jesus Christ an *amelaj* (intercessor-mediator) when he was on earth? Is he an

---

[2] See Glossary of Amharic Terms for definitions and for Amharic spelling.

intercessor-mediator now? Do you ever pray to Christ? How often? Do you ever pray to anyone else? Who? How often?

Interview Question 9. What kind of relationship would you say you have with Jesus Christ? What human relationship is the best example of the kind of relationship you have with Jesus?

Interview Question 10. How is Jesus Christ related to God the Father? Is Jesus Christ a different person from *Medhane Alem* ("Savior of the World")? Who would you say is greater, Jesus Christ, or the Virgin Mary?

## Analysis of Interview Questions

Interview question one was designed as a "Survey" (Fetterman 1989, 51) or "Grand Tour" question (Spradley 1989, 86) to allow subjects to express what was important to them in their own terminology. This question often led to slight revision in the order in which the following questions were asked or the way in which they were asked. Interview question two was intended to discover if the subject understood these less common Amharic terms for "nature" and "person" differently from the terms commonly used. After the earliest interviews it was determined that only the clergy had any understanding of these terms, and so this question was not usually included when interviewing lay people.

The questions included under number three and number seven are similar to Spradley's "verification questions" and Fetterman's "opened-ended questions" (Spradley 1989, 126-29;

Fetterman 1989, 54). They were included to test hypotheses about how people would understand the concepts of Christ's divinity and humanity, the union (*tewahedo*) of his divinity and humanity, and of Christ's having "one nature" or "two natures." These questions were often modified depending on how the subject answered question one.

Questions four and five were included to further probe into the answers given in questions one, three, and seven; specifically to see how the subject dealt with examples from the Bible in which Jesus seemed to act explicitly as a human being. They arose out of the historical and formal emphasis of the Orthodox church that Christ never acted simply as a human or simply as divine.

During the first few interviews it became apparent that many subjects felt that Christ's nature was different after he was resurrected and ascended to heaven than when he walked the earth. Interview question six was added to explore the way people perceived that Christ's nature had changed. As with questions four and five, this question was included to probe more deeply into the answers given by the subject to questions one, three, and seven.

The operational question which sought to determine subjects' perspective on their relationship with Christ was developed in interview questions eight and nine. The question about whether Christ was an *amelaj* (intercessor-mediator) was initially suggested by Dr. Seeyoum Gebre Selassie and proved crucial in understanding subjects' own frame of reference on Christ's nature. It also served as a form of "contrast question" providing triangulation to confirm subjects' understanding of how Christ's nature was similar and different to that of other beings (Spradley 1989, 160-69; Fetterman 1989, 89-92). The questions on prayer further explicated the subjects' understanding of Christ's role as an intercessor-mediator.

Question nine on subjects' relationship (Amharic: *genunyenet*) with Christ was usually the final question, and again allowed subjects to use their own frame of reference to talk about how they understood the person of Christ. Question nine also served to gauge subjects' sense of distance from Christ, and so provided a further point of triangulation with previous questions to determine subjects' sense of Christ's imminence and transcendence.

Questions listed under the tenth interview question were asked infrequently, depending on the answers given in the other questions, and were used to further clarify answers previously given.

## Conduct of Interviews and Recording Interview Results

All interviews were held at a location determined by the subject. Forty-eight interviews were held at either the subject's place of residence, worship, or work.[3] Three interviews were held at the home of the researcher at the request of subjects.

Most interviews were conducted with only the researcher, the subject and (on fourteen occasions) the researcher's translator present. Interviews which were held at subjects' work places or residences were occasionally interrupted briefly by family, friends, or customers who entered the room in which the interview was taking place. During six of the interviews held in residences and three of the interviews held in places of work, family members or work colleagues were present throughout the interviews. In all cases the researcher offered to reschedule the interview for a time and place when the subject could be alone with the researcher, but in all cases the subject insisted that the presence of others was acceptable. Four of the interviews which were held with clergy at the Gebre Kristos church were held in the presence of younger students who were preparing to be deacons at the church. In all four cases these young students were present with the approval of the subject. In three of these cases the presence of these younger students did not appear to affect the subjects' answers. In one case, the subject twice altered his answers, apparently based on the

---

[3]These forty-eight interviews include thirteen held in the compound of the Gebre Kristos church. In five cases--two restaurant/bars, two beauty salons, and one cotton-spinning "factory"--the front room of the subject's residence was also the subject's place of work.

presence of these students. The altered answers were noted in the researcher's notes and considered during the analysis of the interviews.

With one exception, each subject was interviewed independently; no two subjects were interviewed at the same time, in the presence of other subjects. The only exception was a husband and wife who were interviewed at the same time. Each was asked the same questions, and the answers for each were noted separately. The validity of these as two independent interviews and two independent subjects was confirmed in that different answers were often given to the same question and one spouse occasionally contradicted the answers given by the other spouse. In violation of traditional Ethiopian culture, the wife occasionally contradicted answers given by her husband.

All interviews were begun with the researcher asking background questions about the subject's life. Two questions were asked to confirm that the subject was indeed a part of the target population. First, each subject was asked to confirm that he or she was then a resident of the Alert/Gebre Kristos neighborhood. Second, each subject was asked to confirm that his or her religion was Ethiopian Orthodox. All subjects were asked about the frequency of their attendance at Orthodox churches in general and at Gebre Kristos Church in particular. All subjects indicated at least occasional attendance at Gebre Kristos Church. In addition, subjects were usually asked about the place of their birth, when they came to live in the Gebre Kristos neighborhood, their family, and about their current occupation. These background questions were found to be especially effective in helping subjects to relax and share more openly with the researcher, especially subjects who were somewhat suspicious about the interview topic.

After asking background questions, the researcher asked each subject the questions listed on the instrument. The exact questions asked and the order of the questions varied according to the interview. Interviews continued until the researcher felt that the subject had explained as much as possible of his or her perspective on the nature of Christ. The duration of the interviews was between twenty minutes and one hour and a half. The average interview with clergy lasted close to an hour, with men about forty-five minutes and with women about thirty minutes.

In order to place subjects at ease and to encourage more honest answers, interviews were conducted as conversations, without the use of any electronic recording devices. The researcher kept brief notes during all interviews. On a number of occasions, when subjects' answers were particularly insightful, the researcher took extensive shorthand notes of verbatim quotations. Immediately after the interview and the separation of researcher and subject, the researcher recorded the subject's responses on a small tape recorder. This verbal summary of the interview was recorded in field notes later the same day. These field notes were analyzed and form the basis of the findings.

In addition to recording the subjects' answers to the questions on the instrument, the researcher also recorded on the field notes subjects' comments, his own comments, and his own interpretations of what he was observing and hearing. Subjects' comments were those offered by the subject before the researcher had asked his first question or which arose due to some circumstance apart from one of the questions on the instrument. These comments were valuable in allowing subjects to establish their own categories of importance. The researcher's comments were those concerning the setting which may have influenced the subjects' answers. Interpretations were the researcher's and/or his translator-assistant's immediate understanding of a subject's answer beyond the answer which was explicitly given.

## Analysis of Field Notes

Field notes were analyzed with the help of the Ethnograph data-base computer program. The process of analysis was primarily a process of triangulation and a search for patterns. First, answers given to the questions on the instrument, comments, and interpretations were analyzed in relation to the particular subject who was speaking. Second, common themes and answers seen in all the interviews were identified. Third, these common themes were coded. Fourth, similarities and dissimilarities were noted among subjects. Responses and attitudes which were held in common were first noted and analyzed in relation to the particular subject; responses and attitudes which appeared to be unique were then noted and analyzed in relation to the particular subject.

Triangulation (Fetterman 1989, 89) was implemented between different subjects, between the different answers given by each individual subject, and between subjects, written literature, and interviews with individuals who were not subjects but who could provide outside perspective on subjects' ideas. Throughout the process of analysis, emerging patterns were tested through triangulation. The patterns which have been tested and found to give the best explanation of the data are the findings of the ethnographic study.

## Overview of Procedure

Emic description of what Ethiopian Orthodox in one urban community think about the nature of Christ began with the researcher defining operational questions based on issues that have emerged through history and present official statements of the Orthodox Church. An interview instrument was prepared based on these operational questions. Based on expected levels of formal religious education, three distinct groups were specified from within the population: laywomen, laymen, and clergy. Subjects were initially selected from among Ethiopian Orthodox with whom the researcher was familiar. These subjects and others helped the researcher make contact with other subjects with whom the interviewer had had no previous contact. The results of these interviews were recorded in field notes which served as the basis of ethnographic analysis. Analysis was based on triangulation and a search for patterns within the answers of each subject and between subjects. These patterns crystallized into findings on popular perspectives on the nature of Christ among Ethiopian Orthodox in one Addis Ababa neighborhood.

CHAPTER 5

FINDINGS

Christological theologizing in Ethiopia demands an understanding of the historical development of Christology in Ethiopia, of Amharic and Ge'ez terms used to talk about Christ, and of official Christological teachings of the Ethiopian Orthodox Church. However, understanding these historical, linguistic and formal perspectives on the nature of Christ are not enough; unless theologians understand popular perceptions of the nature of Christ they risk beginning their theology at the wrong place. To help in determining popular perspectives on the nature of Christ in the Ethiopian Orthodox Church, an ethnographic study has been conducted in one neighborhood in Addis Ababa. Findings from that study form an important part of the framework for Christological theologizing among the people of that neighborhood.

## The "Nature" of Christ

Subjects were initially asked a general question about how they understood Christ's "nature"[1] to discover categories

---

[1] The Amharic words *baheriy* and *tebay* were both used in the question. See the Glossary of Amharic terms.

and terminology that would emerge before the researcher asked more specific questions. Subjects gave a wide variety of responses to this general question.[2] Some spoke of what they understood to be the most important principles of Ethiopian Orthodoxy. Others began talking about various works of Christ. Several emphasized that Christ's nature was beyond understanding. A few, particularly clergy, shared their understanding of Christ's ontological character.

## Christ's Nature Described as Ethiopian Orthodoxy

When asked about the nature of Christ, some subjects did not talk about the person of Jesus Christ at all. Instead, they responded to the question about Christ's *baheriy* by talking about what was important to them regarding Ethiopian Orthodoxy. One woman said that she attended church regularly, greeted the church,[3] and believed that God is one. Another woman, a young widow, responded that she tried to

---

[2] Five women indicated that they did not understand the words *baheriy* and *tebay*. Four of these, however, understood enough of the question to say something about Christ. Three said something about Christ granting salvation, and the fourth said that Christ was her creator and protector. Their responses indicated that they understood the words for "nature" enough to describe who Christ was. The fifth woman said that all she knew was that God protected and provided for her and she believed "what the old fathers [of the church] have passed down." Her answered indicated that she may not have understood the words for "nature" at all.

[3] The EOC teaches that its members should give "greetings" to every Orthodox church building whenever they pass it because it houses the holy ark of God (*tabot*). These greetings are given by nodding the head in the direction of the church in genuflection.

separate herself from sin; she had made a vow not to marry again, but to live her life dedicated to God.

Several men responded by talking about the intercessor-mediators (*amalajoch*). An older man responded that all religions were different branches growing out of the same tree; what distinguished Ethiopian Orthodoxy was its emphasis on the *amalajoch* who receive their authority from God. Another man initially was perplexed by the question, then said that the EOC believed in God as creator, the *amalajoch* and fasting. A young deacon said that the foundation of Ethiopian Orthodoxy was not just Christ, but all the "saints of old" (*qedusan*), including Mary, the angels, and the apostles. Throughout the Bible, he said, it can be seen that they interceded to God on behalf of others.

## Beyond Understanding

A number of subjects, particularly laymen and clergy, initially emphasized that Christ and his nature were beyond human understanding, and so they could not properly answer questions about his nature. One older man said that "Christ can't be seen or touched, so how can we know his nature?" A younger man gave his explanation of Christ as God clothed in human flesh who came to earth to suffer for mankind, but quickly added, "the mystery of Christ is very deep; it is not something that can be examined."[4] Another man said that Christ cannot be known through science or reasoning, but only through the sacred writings. Several women said that they had not been educated and so these things were beyond them.

Clergy were particularly inclined to emphasize that Christ's nature could not be known or understood. Three priests emphasized that Christ could not be examined closely. One of those priests twice repeated that Christ was distant, and could not be known, and another said that he was "beyond comprehension." He added, "Without being here, he came here," indicating that, in Christ, God came to earth, but that in his presence on earth the mysteries of who he was were not revealed. A monk said that Christ "could not been seen or touched." After emphasizing that Christ was distant and cannot be examined, one priest began talking about how people could be restored to God and obtain his favor through the intercessor/mediators (*amalajoch*). When clergy responded that Christ's nature was beyond human understanding they often added a warning that these spiritual matters should not be probed too deeply.

---

[4] Subjects' quotations throughout Chapter 5 are the researcher's own translation of subjects' responses based on shorthand notes taken by the researcher during interviews. Every attempt was made to record and translate as closely as possible to a verbatim quotation, but because both the recording of the notes and the translation process were inevitably imperfect, quotations should be considered as very close renderings of what subjects actually said.

## The Work of Christ: Savior, Example and Teacher

Many subjects, particularly women, explained their understanding of Christ's "nature" by talking about Christ's works. Christ was explained as being primarily savior, example and teacher. One woman said, "Christ was born to die. He was crucified to be our savior . . . . He helped the poor and was an example to us as to how we should help the poor and those in need." Another woman, interviewed the week before Easter, responded that, "Christ came to earth and fasted for forty days as an example to us. He suffered and died for us, as we honor this week. Shouldn't we fast forty days as well?" A younger woman said, "Christ was savior and teacher. He came to lead us in the right way and to lead us to the Father." Two younger women responded to the question about Christ's nature by telling the story of mankind, beginning with the creation. After God created human beings, they fell into sin. So God made a covenant with Adam to save people from their sin. Jesus was born to fulfill that covenant. His body was broken and his blood was shed; he died, arose, and ascended, so all people could pass from death to life. Another women gave an equally long answer, describing Jesus' life and death in detail and mentioning that he came to save people from the sin of Adam and Eve. A total of eleven women mentioned something about Jesus being crucified and/or being Savior in answer to the question about Christ's nature.

Many laymen also explained Christ's nature by saying he was savior and example. One man said that he was an example in being baptized and in fasting. A man summarized the responses of many when he said that Christ was born to teach, fast, be crucified and be resurrected to forgive sin. He became a man for the purpose of doing these works. Another man immediately referred to the creation, Adam's fall into sin and a prophecy God then gave to Adam. Christ was born of a virgin, taught, and was crucified, he said, to fulfill that prophecy. A teenage boy who had regularly attended teaching sessions at the Gebre Kristos Church described Christ's life on earth, including his teaching and healing ministries and his death and resurrection to forgive sins, but emphasized Christ's present power to change lives.

> Christ has done powerful work among the people of this community. Many young troublemakers (*dureeoch*) who drank, stole and caused all kinds of problems have received Christ now and turned into preachers of Christ. This could only come from the savior's power.

One man also emphasized Christ's present saving and protecting work: "Christ is for us, and we need to bow in worship to him. He controls the nations. He destroys evil men. His is powerful and in control."

Clergy were less likely to refer to Christ's works as savior and example when asked about his nature. However, some did refer to his being born, beaten, and crucified to save. One priest added that "he broke bread on our behalf." After quoting John 6:54[5] he said, "In this way he became savior for the sons of men. He was redeemer and reconciler . . . . By coming into the world he brought light into the darkness."

### Christ's Ontological Character

Women did not usually answer questions about the "nature" of Christ by speaking about his ontological character. One mentioned that he was God's son. Another responded by saying that she believed that there was one God. Another said that because the Virgin Mary was Jesus' mother that he himself was God.

Several men explained the nature of Christ by describing his ontological character through his life and work. A middle-aged layman with a reputation for being well educated in Orthodox teaching responded by explaining the Trinity. The EOC believes in Father, Son, and Holy Spirit. Christ is the Son, who is God's messenger to earth. He was born as a man by the Virgin Mary and was "seen by those who would see him and not seen by those who would not see him." He seemed to be saying that Christ's nature as God's Son could only be perceived by those with faith. An older man, also with a reputation for being strong in his faith, said that Christ was "fully God, like a man," and that he was born, grew, taught, fasted, suffered, was crucified and resurrected. A younger man asserted that Christ was "God clothed in human

---

[5] "Whoever eats my flesh and drinks my blood remains in me, and I in him."

flesh, who came to suffer and do the work that needed to be done for humans." Another man said that he was God, descended from heaven to earth, born of the Virgin Mary, who performed miracles and who did everything a person does except for sin. His flesh was broken and blood was spilled to save people from Sheol. He emphasized that "he was not crucified in his divinity, but to save us from sin," stressing both Christ's full humanity (he died) and the reason for his humanity (to save humans). His answer also indicated a willingness to say Christ did something (die) apart from his divine nature.

The clearest and most forceful connection of Christ's person and works among laymen came from a middle-aged man who immediately responded that Christ

> had two natures, a divine nature and a human nature. Certain things happened to Christ that couldn't happen to God: he was crucified, was tired, was beaten. Certain things happened to Christ that couldn't happen to a man: he commanded others, he had authority over the world, he healed, he saved. So he had both a divine and a human nature.[6]

Clergy frequently answered questions about Christ's "nature" by referring to who he was ontologically. Several began with an explanation of the Trinity.[7] One deacon, who

---

[6] As will be seen, this man's response was not typical, not only in giving an answer which described the ontological character of Christ, but also in his understanding of Christ as having "two natures" when on earth.

[7] In answers to subsequent questions, two additional clergy and one layman said Christ was the same nature, spirit, or divinity as the Father and Holy Spirit. One added that he had a different person (*akal*).

subsequently achieved the status of *meri-gaeta*,[8] gave a lengthy explanation of the Council of Nicea and its teachings on the Trinity. The Father is the heart of God, the Son the Word of God, and the Spirit the breath of God, he asserted. Christ was the Son, born of the Virgin Mary. It is "Orthodox" to continue in the true faith of these Nicean fathers. This deacon stressed the deity of Christ and his oneness with the Father. Two priests also gave answers which explained the nature of Christ in relation to God the Father and God the Holy Spirit, one adding that Christ was "Creator, God". A few clergy made no distinction between "Christ" and the "Trinity." A debtara and a monk both said that "Christ is one in three and three in one."

Several clergy emphasized Christ's unchanging deity and oneness with the other members of the Trinity in his incarnation. A deacon responded that

> Christ was God. God's nature was Christ's nature and Christ's nature was God's nature. God is three persons, but one nature. Christ became a man, but his divine nature did not change.

A monk said simply, "The word became flesh. God became man." A priest emphasized that "Christ was the creator. He was who he was before he came to earth." He went on to stress that his divinity was unchanged when he was on earth. A debtara said that Christ had "one nature. It could not change. It is the same as God the Father's nature. He was divine." A

---

[8]See page 14 and Glossary of Amharic Terms.

priest affirmed that Christ was God, but that he "was born of Saint Virgin Mary [and] took on human flesh to be the savior of the world. There was a union (*tewahedo*) of his divinity and flesh."

## Summary

Subjects were initially asked about their general "understanding the nature of Christ," to allow them to express ideas in their own categories of thought. A few women did not understand the Amharic words for nature. Some subjects did not mention the person of Jesus Christ; they spoke of fasting, celibacy, and the intercessor/mediators--things that were important to them in the Orthodox faith. Others, particularly laymen and clergy, objected that the nature of Christ was beyond human understanding, so they could not truly understand it or explain it. Many subjects, especially, women, responded by talking about Christ's works as savior, example, and teacher. Laymen frequently described Christ as God and man as seen in his works on earth. Clergy were likely to begin explaining Christ's nature by referring the Trinity and Christ's relationship to the other members of the Trinity. Some clergy went on to explain Christ's incarnation, stressing his unchanging deity and oneness with the Father when he was a human being.

## God, Man or God-Man When on Earth?

Most of those interviewed agreed that when Christ was on earth he was in some sense both God and man. However, many of those who believed he was both God and man seemed to understand his humanity as something different from that of other human beings. A few subjects insisted that Christ was only God when he was on earth, and three laymen said that he was only man.

### Both God and Man

Most subjects agreed that Christ was in some way both God and man when he was on earth. Some felt that Christ's humanity was a true, genuine humanity. However, many subjects seemed to believe that Christ's humanity was in some way different from that of other people, that he was not *genuinely* human. Many seemed to fear that asserting Christ's full humanity would detract from his deity, and they were unwilling to do this.

## The Nature of the Incarnation

Subjects explained the union of deity and humanity in Christ in two ways: through theological expressions that explained how God could become man and by talking about works of Christ which proved he was both God and man.

### Theological Expressions for the Incarnation

The most common expression used by subjects to describe the union of Christ's divinity and humanity was that he was "God clothed in flesh."⁹ Many described the union of Christ's divinity and humanity as taking place in the womb of the Virgin Mary, with Christ taking her human flesh.¹⁰ A young layman explained, "As a person is created, Christ was created in the womb of Mary." This same man repeated three times that Christ was God "clothed in human flesh." A young priest described Christ's divine conception in the womb of the Virgin Mary as being like sunlight coming through a glass window, bringing light and heat. He was conceived by God, so he was God; he was conceived in the womb of Mary, so he was man. An older man said that Christ was "divine, clothed in flesh. His divinity was unchanging, but flesh was added to it."

Laymen and clergy often used the word "*tewahedo*" ("union") to describe the relationship of Christ's divinity and humanity.¹¹ A deacon specified that in the *tewahedo* "two

---

[9] This phrase was used by four women, four laymen, and two members of the clergy. An additional two layman and four members of the clergy said that Christ "took human flesh." The frequent use of these phrases by subjects probably indicates that they are used commonly by clergy or in other Ethiopian Orthodox settings, so that even less educated lay people become familiar with them.

[10] Two women, eight laymen, and eight members of the clergy referred to the union of Christ's divinity and humanity in Mary's womb or said that Christ received his flesh and/or humanity from Mary.

[11] The word "*tewahedo*" was used to explain the union of Christ's divinity and humanity by four laymen, and five clergy. As with "clothed in human flesh," the frequent use of "*tewahedo*" by less educated people probably indicates that it is heard repeatedly in church and other Orthodox contexts; lay people may simply know that they believe in *tewahedo* and may

natures became one . . . . God became perfect man in one nature and one person in Mary's womb." An older layman explained *tewahedo* by saying that Christ was of the seed of Adam and the seed of David, joined with deity in Mary's womb. "How can you explain this! God is the creator of things and Christ was created in Mary's womb the same way other things are created." A young deacon compared the *tewahedo* union of Christ's deity and humanity to putting a piece of metal into a fire. "The fire makes it red hot, and there is a union of heat and metal into one."

A debtara explained *tewahedo* by contrasting it with what he understood to be the opposite theological position: *Qebat*.[12]

> The union of Christ's divinity and humanity was the union of spirit and flesh, the spirit from God and the flesh from Mary, joined in the womb of the virgin Mary. The *Tewahedo* believe there was this union of spirit and flesh but the *Qebat* say that there was not a union but an anointing. But when you anoint something, there's not real union. For example, when a person anoints himself with butter[13] he is simply covering himself. There is no real union between himself and the butter.

*Tewahedo*, he said, describes a true, organic union of human flesh and divine spirit, not simply an outward covering of Christ's divinity with humanity. A second debtara also

---

not understand the word's precise theological meaning.

[12]"Anointing." See pages 80-81 and Appendix A for the historical background and an explanation of the differences between the *Tewahedo* and *Qebat* positions on the anointing of Christ.

[13]Ethiopians sometimes spread butter over their skin or hair for purposes of health or beauty.

contrasted the *Tewahedo* with the *Qebat* and used the illustration of anointing with butter. He added that in the same way that oil and water do not mix, the *Qebat* believe that Christ "did not merge with the flesh of Mary." However, he believed that there was a true union (*tewahedo*) between Christ and Mary's flesh.

The Divine-Human Works of the God-Man

Some subjects described things that Christ did in order to show that he was both God and man when on earth. As God he performed miracles—especially healing—and forgave sin.[14] As man he was born, grew, taught other people, ate and drank, fasted, was baptized, suffered and died. One deacon told the story of Jesus healing a blind man by making clay and breathing into it divine breath. As man he made the clay; as God he healed the man through divine breath. A young deacon said that "As man he grew; as God he didn't need to grow." One older man said, "Christ was divine, and divinity cannot change. He took on flesh to teach, to die, and to forgive sins. That is why he became a man: to do these works."

In particular, subjects explained that in the incarnation Christ had to come as both God and man in order to provide salvation for mankind. Four women explained the union of Christ's divinity and humanity by saying that the divine

---

[14] Besides the miracle stories in the canonical Scriptures, one man told the story of Christ making a bird out of clay and giving it life when he was a boy.

Christ had to also become a man in order to die to save people from sin. A deacon described the sin of Adam and Eve which doomed the human race to live in sin. Quoting Romans 5:12[15] he explained that Christ had to be both God and man in order to save humans from that sin.

Other subjects stressed that Christ had to become a man in order to teach and serve as an example to human beings. Two women and one layman said that Christ had to become a man in order to teach people. Another laymen said that Christ came to teach and "fulfilled all things when he was on earth--fasted, lived a perfect life, honored Sundays--so we should do them as well."

Finally, several subjects explained the incarnation by emphasizing that Christ had to become man to reveal God to human beings. A women commented, "As God, [Christ] was very distant. He could not be examined or touched. Then he came to earth as a person, he could be seen and touched in his person (akal) . . . . He was both God and man." A layman said that Christ "became a man so people would see him. They saw he was a person, but it was clear that he was also God because of his miracles."

---

[15] "Therefore, just as sin entered the world through one man, and death through sin, and in this way death came to all men, because all sinned . . . ."

Summary

Subjects generally felt that Christ was in some sense both God and man. They explained his incarnation both by using theological expressions, such as "God clothed in human flesh" and the union (*tewahedo*) of flesh and spirit, and by explaining that Christ did works that can only be done by God and works that can only be done by man. God had to become a man to save, to teach, to serve as an example, and to reveal himself.

## Truly Divine and Truly Human

Some of the more educated subjects attempted to describe a union which preserved Christ's true divinity and true humanity. One debtara said that Christ was "true man" ("*eunetenya sew*"). An older layman said that Christ was fully God and "exactly human" ("*tekekelenya sew*") but without sin. A middle-aged man affirmed that Christ was "perfect God and perfect man." A middle-aged man with a reputation for knowing Orthodoxy well said that Christ "was fully like a man at every state of humanity." Another layman said that Christ's death was necessary, not only to save, but also to prove he was human. Using a precise Amharic expression, one woman said "holding onto divinity, he became a man (*amlakenet yezo, sew ho-ne*)."[16]

---

[16]The researcher did not hear this expression in any other interview or encounter it in any written sources. It seems to have been this woman's own understanding of the relationship between Christ's divinity and humanity.

Many subjects expressed Christ's humanity by explaining that he had every human experience except sin.[17] A woman said, "Every circumstance that came to people came to him . . . . He felt the same suffering we do." A deacon said that Christ, "had a weak human flesh that hungered, thirsted, and got tired." Another deacon mentioned that John 4 records that Jesus was thirsty. He exclaimed, "Here he was, the creator of water, yet he thirsted and asked for water. He had a weak flesh, a flesh that hungered and thirsted and got tired." When asked if Christ had ever hungered and gotten tired, one man answered, "He hungered powerfully! He got tired like any other man." A priest called Christ a "man of the earth (*miderawey*)" to describe his humanity.

Not Quite *Truly* Human

A number of subjects, however, seemed to feel that, though Christ was both God and man, he was somehow not fully human; most were hesitant to call him "perfect man" or "true man." When asked if Jesus was God or man when on earth, one man responded, "God the creator," followed by silence. When asked if he was also a man, the subject responded that Christ lived *like* a man and died *like* a man but, he also knew what was in their hearts. He had the knowledge of God on the

---

[17]About two-thirds of all subjects agreed that Christ became hungry, thirsty, and tired just as other human beings do.

inside, but he acted like a man on the outside.[18] An older man said that "Christ seemed to come as a man, but we believe he was God clothed in flesh to die. God is God. God is spirit." His idea seems to have been that Christ was spiritual God on the inside but human flesh on the outside. When asked if Christ was God, man or both, a woman responded that he "taught as if he was God." When pressed with whether or not he was also man, the woman responded,

> That is a "thing of the mouth (*afenya neger;* something which is rumored)." He was born of the virgin Mary, and because of his birth of Mary, it was *said* that he was man. When those who were poor or in distress or suffering came to Mary, she was very sympathetic and would respond to their need.

This woman could not bring herself to say that Jesus was truly human; she found greater comfort in the genuine humanity of Mary.

At least one priest doubted that Christ was fully human. He said that Christ "took the image of man to teach us and show us how to live. But he was true God, *not* true man (*eunetenya sew*)." This same priest was shocked at the suggestion that Christ could ever have become hungry or tired like an ordinary person.

The tendency to doubt Christ's true humanity was graphically expressed by a sixty year old man who had studied

---

[18]The interviewer's translator was present during this interview. After the interview, the translator said that the subject seemed to think of Christ as a manifestation of God who only appeared to be human but did not have a human soul or full human attributes.

Orthodoxy most of his life. He said that Christ became a man to teach human beings, but that "he didn't come to dig. He didn't come to build a house. He didn't have our human nature (*tebay*). He was our king, above us." It seems that his idea was that Christ was human-like, but that he didn't come to do the common work that humans do.

"Clothed in Flesh"

It seems likely that, though the commonly used expression "God clothed in human flesh" was used by some to imply that Christ was truly human, it was used by others to imply that he was God on the inside with only a human appearance on the outside. On the one hand, an older man said that Christ was "clothed in human flesh" and so was "exactly human." On the other hand, a younger woman affirmed that Christ was "God clothed in flesh," but she was uncomfortable saying he was man. A younger man gave a similar answer: Christ was "God clothed in human flesh," but he would not agree that he was "perfect man." An older man said that though Christ "*seemed* to come as a man, we believe he was God, clothed in flesh to die. God is God; God is spirit." Two women said that in Christ God took on a human *se'el*, a word used to describe a painted picture.

Christ Hungary, Thirsty, or Tired?

The feeling that Christ was not fully human was underscored by the many who felt that he did not truly become hungry, thirsty, or tired when he was on earth. Though about two-thirds of all subjects agreed that Christ experienced these human weaknesses, many, particularly women, insisted that because Christ was God, he could not hunger, thirst or get tired. One woman insisted that Christ never became hungry through his forty days of fasting. Several said that he only appeared to become hungry, thirsty and tired in order to teach others how to endure this hardships or to prove who he was through testing.[19] When asked if Christ ever got hungry, thirsty, or tired, one woman responded,

> How could he? He had all authority. He had no pain, he had no hunger. He feeds us so how could he become hungry. There was one time during the "time of pain", the 40 days of fasting before Easter, when he fasted. But he was not hungry like us, though he was passing through the time of hunger. But he only fasted like this to teach us to fast, not because he really was hungry.

Another woman answered, "Only to be tested. He himself was the creator," implying that since he was God, he could not truly be weak. The older man who said that Christ had not "come to earth to dig," incredulously responded, "Christ hungry, tired?! No! Remember how he used five loaves and two fishes to make food for many thousands of people," implying that anyone with divine power would never suffer hunger.

---

[19] Eight women, three laymen, and one clergy said that Christ did not truly become hungry, thirsty, or tired in the same way that other people do, and two women said they were too uncertain to answer the question. Seven subjects said that the purpose of Christ's apparent weaknesses was to teach his followers; three said his apparent weaknesses were only to test him.

Another man said that Christ lived "without getting worn out" ("*alselechem*").

Some of those who agreed that Christ did experience true human hunger, thirst, and tiredness emphasized that it was only to teach people how to suffer, be merciful, and be humble. One man agreed that Christ experienced suffering when he was beaten and when Satan tempted him, "but he was untroubled on the inside."

Divine Humanity

Several subjects indicated that they believed that, though Christ was both divine and human, his humanity was a divine humanity. One layman and four clergy repeated the formula "God became man and man became God" to describe the incarnation. The idea of this phrase is that the union of the incarnation was so complete that Christ's humanity was made a divine humanity. A debtara emphasized that Christ's divinity and humanity were united into one nature such that "his flesh itself was divine," an explicitly Apollinarian idea which the EOC officially rejects. By emphasizing that Christ's humanity was a divine humanity, these subjects demonstrated a tendency to see Christ's humanity as essentially different from that of other people.

The Time of Christ's Return

Most subjects were asked how they understood Christ's remarks when he was asked the time of the Son of Man's return, and responded that only the Father in heaven knew. One of the purposes of this question was to determine if subjects understood this as a time when Christ acted as a human being, apart from any divine attributes. With the exception of three laymen who maintained that Christ was only an exalted human,[20] only one laymen and three clergy suggested that this was a time when Christ was acting as a human being. All three clergy responded that he was speaking "in his flesh" at this time.[21] The only layman to suggest that Christ had two natures--one human and one divine--said that his answer to the question of the time of his return demonstrated that he was a perfect man.

All remaining subjects who answered this question[22] gave answers which indicated that Christ really did know the time of the Son of man's return to earth. Two answers were especially common. First, four women, four men and five clergy said that Christ really knew when he was returning, but he was telling the disciples that the time of his return was God's matter, which must remain a mystery to them. Second,

---

[20] See below page 143.

[21] All three clergy consistently maintained Christ's true humanity throughout their interviews. By answering that Christ said something "in his flesh" these three clergy demonstrate that some EOC clergy are willing to say that Christ performed some actions only in his humanity. See the subject's comment on page 141 and footnotes 23 and 24 for examples of subjects expressing the opinion that Christ did not act strictly in his humanity.

[22] Fourteen women, twelve laymen, and nine clergy.

five women, five men, and one clergy said that Christ really did know the time of his return, but he told them that the Son of man didn't know in order to honor his Father and draw attention to the Father's power and wisdom.[23]

The large majority of subjects who maintained that Christ really did know the time of his return further verify that many subjects felt that in some way Christ was not fully or genuinely human.[24]

## Summary

Most subjects felt that Christ was both divine and human. He was God clothed in human flesh. His nature was a true union of divinity and deity. He actions on earth demonstrate that he was both God and man.

However many subjects also felt that in some way Christ was less than truly or genuinely human. Some subjects implied that Christ was God on the inside, but human on the outside, and some subjects expressly denied that Christ's humanity was like that of other people. Some did not feel that he was ever hungry, thirsty, or tired in the same way

---

[23] In addition: two women and two clergy said Christ was telling them they were at fault to ask this question; one man and one woman said Christ was sidestepping the question to avoid sin; one woman said he was testing the disciples; one man said he was telling them that they should already know the answer to this question; one man said he avoided answering to hide his deity; and one member of the clergy said that he was trying to get them to understand their need for God.

[24] In addition, these answers help verify that few Ethiopian Orthodox would say that Christ ever acted strictly "in his humanity."

other people are. Some felt that his humanity was a special, divine humanity. Very few suggested that in his humanity he did not know the time of his return to earth.

## Only God

Several subjects[25] affirmed quite strongly that Christ was only God and was not a man when he was on earth. Women were more likely than laymen or priests to feel that Christ was only God. One woman asked, "How could he be a man? He is God. Is not God deity (*Igziabeher amlak aydelem*)?" When asked if Christ was God, man, or both God and man, another woman initially answered with confusion, but later insisted that he could not have had a human nature. He only had the nature of God. Another woman affirmed, "He was God, the creator. How could he be a man? He was only God." When asked if Christ was "true God and true man," one woman responded, "True God" followed by an emphatic silence.

## Only Man

While most subjects affirmed the deity and humanity of Christ, with a tendency to limit or deny his true humanity, three laymen took a very different viewpoint. They said that Christ was not God in any sense when he was on earth. He was only a great man who was similar to other intercessor-mediators (*amalajoch*). One said, "We believe in God by Mary,

---

[25] Five women and one layman specifically stated that Christ was only God, and was in no sense a man, when he was on earth.

Michael, and Gabriel, the messengers of God. Christ was a messenger of God, an intercessor-mediator (*amalaj*) of God." One of these men admitted that he only occasionally attended church and was not a very good Christian. Another was a younger, progressive government official, and may have been reflecting the Marxist-oriented education he had received as he was growing up. These three subjects were consistent throughout their interviews in their understanding that Christ had only one human nature and that he was neither more or less than other intercessor-mediators honored by the Ethiopian Orthodox Church.

### Summary: The God-Man, But Less than Truly Man

Though a handful of subjects felt that Christ was only God or only man when he was on earth, most agreed that he was, in some sense, both human and divine. Most also agreed that, as a man, he got hungry, thirsty, and tired. However there was a strong tendency to limit his humanity in some way. Many implied that he was God on the inside and human on the outside. Others said that he did not experience true human weaknesses. A few stated or implied that his humanity was a divine humanity, unlike that of other people. Many were hesitant to say that he was "true man." Over half of all subjects either did not believe Christ was human or seemed to place some limitation on his humanity.

### God or Man Now?

Most subjects felt that Christ's nature changed after his resurrection and his ascension from earth to heaven. All seventeen women who were asked whether Christ was now God, man, or both God and man affirmed that he was now only God. One woman who hesitated to answer most of the questions emphatically answered, "Only God!"

Seventeen men were also asked about Christ's present nature, and thirteen said that he was now only God. One man explained that Christ's saving work was completed when he was on earth, and so he was now no longer man. Another said that Christ was now only God because "his suffering is done." Another tried to prove that Christ was now only God because he sent the Holy Spirit to earth. Obviously one who had the authority to send the Holy Spirit must be only God. The three men who believed that Christ was only a man when he was on earth felt he was now an exalted man of some sort, but that he was certainly not God now. Only one layman felt that Christ was now both God and man.

Six clergy felt that Christ was now only God and five felt that he was both God and man. One deacon made a direct connection between Christ's present divine nature and his not being an intercessor-mediator (*amalaj*). "Christ is not now a man; if he was, he could be an intercessor-mediator. But he is not now a man, so he cannot now be an intercessor-mediator." One priest and one deacon agreed that Christ must still be the god-man because of the importance of the union (*tewahedo*) of his divinity and humanity. For these two clergy the question of Christ's present nature was a chance to emphasize the complete union of Christ's natures.

In summary, laypeople generally believed that since his resurrection and ascension Jesus Christ is no longer human in any sense, but only divine. Clergy, on the other hand, were divided in how they understood Christ's present nature. Their understanding of Christ's present nature was dependent on other theological issues, such as whether or not he is an intercessor-mediator.

## How Many Natures?

The large majority of subjects strongly believed that Jesus Christ had only one nature.[26] A belief that Christ had only one nature grew from a desire to ensure Christ's deity, from a concern that saying he had two natures implied that he was divided against himself, and from a feeling that speaking of one nature best preserved the union of Christ's person taught by the Ethiopian Orthodox Church. Four subjects were unsure of how many natures Christ had, or were vague in their answers. On the other hand, ten subjects responded positively to the idea that Christ had two natures.

---

[26]The Amharic word "*baheriy*" was used in the question. The word "*tebay*" was sometimes added for clarification.

## Only One Nature

Thirty-six subjects felt that Christ could only have one nature.[27] One debtara responded to the initial question about Christ's nature by saying, "He had one nature," signifying the importance of the single nature of Christ to him. Some simply rejected the idea that he could have two natures, but would not give any reason why they felt that way.[28] Many, however, gave reasons why they believed Christ could only have one nature.

### Christ was Essentially God

Some subjects felt Christ could only have one nature because he was essentially God, and his divine nature could not change. To suggest that he had a second nature would imply that he was less than God. One woman simply responded, "He had a divine nature!" to the suggestion that Christ might have had two natures. An older woman asked, "How can God have two natures. He's God!" Later in the conversation it became apparent that she was afraid that if she talked about two natures, she might be implying that Christ was, in some sense, only a man; then she might be accused of being too much like

---

[27] This is 72% of those who answered the question on how they would respond to someone who said that Christ had two natures.

[28] Sample answers from women: "I reject that." "It's not possible [for him to have two natures]." From men: "No, one nature. He cannot have two." "There is only one Christ." From a monk: "One nature, not two! Be careful in asking these questions!"

the Muslims. Because Christ was first and foremost God, he could not have a second, human nature. Another woman explained that "God's nature and man's nature are different. Christ had one nature, though he came to be tested as man and to show himself as God. He had only one nature." Because human and divine natures are incompatible, and because Christ was essentially God, he must have had only one, divine nature. A woman who was unsure of many of her answers emphatically asked, "How can Christ have two natures? He can only have one nature . . . . His nature is the nature of God."

Several men also argued that Christ was essentially God, and so could not have two natures. One man who had earlier insisted that Christ was both God and man demonstrated that Christ only took the *appearance* of a man, and so did not have a human nature.

> No, two not natures. Two natures were not clearly revealed. Christ's humanity is like this wood [At this point he tapped on the wood post of his porch]. If this wood took on the appearance of a person, it would still be wood, though it would look like a person on the outside. Christ didn't have two natures. He had to appear as a human being because of the Jews' doubt and rejection.

It seems that this man conceived of Christ as a person on the outside but as deity on the inside. In his essential, inward character he was only God. Another man who had also explained that Christ was both God and man, later clarified that "Christ *seemed* to come as a man, but we believe he was God clothed in flesh. God is God, spirit." Christ was God, and so it could never be said that he had a human nature. His humanity must be limited to his outward, fleshly clothes. A man who had hesitated to say that Christ was a man when on earth, insisted that Christ had "one nature, a divine nature."

## Christ Could Not Be Divided Against Himself

Many subjects argued that Christ could have only one nature because saying he had two natures would imply that he was divided against himself. One woman answered, "How can God have many thoughts? It's not possible." A man responded that "Christ's conduct cannot be split into two." Developing an elaborate anthropology, a priest said, "No, he has only one nature and one thought. People have many thoughts, many natures; they have seven natures. Not Christ. He has only one nature."[29]

At least three subjects brought together the idea that Christ was essentially God and that his mind could not be divided against itself in their rejection of his having two natures. Two of these subjects were older laymen who were considered well-educated and very faithful to Orthodoxy. One asked,

---

[29] The elaborate anthropology expressed by this man ("people . . . have seven natures") was not encountered elsewhere by the researcher, and deserves further ethnographic and bibliographic research which is beyond the scope of this thesis. Three subjects--one woman, one layman, and one debtara--gave a parallel line of argument, saying that Christ could only have one nature (*baheriy*) because he only had one person (*akal*).

> How can God change? "Two natures" implies change. A nature is what a person thinks, his actions, his purpose, his direction, his mind, his way of thinking (*astesasab*). These were one in Christ, and so his nature was one.

Christ was essentially God, and since God cannot change or contradict himself, he could not have had two natures. The other layman had a very similar line of argument.

> How can a person have two natures in his one stomach? A person cannot be divided in his nature. His nature comes from his circumstances and the place he lives. His nature is known from his deeds. Christ was like one farmer plowing with two bulls. God's nature cannot change. A person's nature can and does change as he grows.

In his example of the farmer, this man seemed to be saying that Christ was both divine and human, but with one will or direction, and hence with only one nature. Christ had a unified nature which could not change because he was essentially God.

The third subject to bring together Christ's essential deity and his single mindset was a priest who responded that

> He only had one nature, not two. There is only one God, and so [Christ] had only one nature. It's the most important thing that he has only one nature. There is only one divinity. He has only one way of thinking (*astesasab*).

There is only one God and Christ was God. Therefore, for this priest, to imply that Christ had two natures would imply that God was divided against himself.

## The EOC Understanding Preserves Christ's Unity

Laypeople rarely said that they believed Christ had one nature because that is the creed of the Ethiopian Orthodox

Church or because it maintained the unity of his person. Clergy, however, had a much clearer understanding of the historical and theological issues involved and frequently mentioned that they believed in one nature because that was the teaching of the EOC and that was the teaching which best preserved the unity of Christ's person. One debtara said, "This is the view of others" when asked how he would respond to someone who said that Christ had two natures. A deacon who was a frequent teacher at the Gebre Kristos church responded by explaining EOC teaching on the incarnation.

> The two natures became one in the womb of Mary. There was a uniting (*tewahedo*) of the two and they became one. Our church does not accept the doctrine of two natures. This is outside of our church.

Both the union of natures and the accepted belief of the EOC were important reasons for this deacon to reject two natures in Christ. Several priests gave answers that were very similar. One asked, "How could God take a nature that was not divine?" A deacon insisted, "No, he doesn't have two natures. That might destroy the idea of the unity of his divinity and humanity."

Another deacon was even more explicit when asked how he would respond to someone who suggested that Christ could have two natures.

> No! The two became one. The Catholics talk about the two natures of Christ. They will say that Christ did certain things in his flesh and certain things in his deity, but we reject that. We believe the two natures were joined into one.

Not only did this deacon reject two natures as the teaching of the (non-Orthodox) Catholics; he explicitly rejected the idea that Christ might have performed certain actions only in his deity or only in his humanity, an idea often closely connected to two-nature Christology and considered theologically dangerous by non-Chalcedonians.[30]

The most extensive theological response to the suggestion that Christ might have had two natures came from the deacon who subsequently became a *meri-gaeta*.

> That's what the Catholics believe and teach. Remember what I told you about the Council of Nicea? There were three Councils in which all the churches agreed. Then came the Council of Chalcedon, when the church split apart. The Catholics divided over this issue, but the Ethiopian Orthodox Church does not accept it. There was Luther, a "mission,"[31] like these *pentis*,[32] who believe this two nature teaching. They follow the teachings of Nestorius.

Several important observations can be made from this answer. First, the deacon was familiar with and strongly rejected the Council of Chalcedon. Second, he branded those who accepted the Council of Chalcedon as Nestorians. Third, he knew that Catholics and evangelicals accepted Chalcedon and so considered them unacceptable to the Ethiopian Orthodox.

---

[30]The large majority of subjects (35) who did not suggest that Christ's ignorance of the time of his return was only in his humanity confirms the reluctance of the Ethiopian Orthodox to suggest that Christ sometimes acted only in his deity and sometimes acted only in his humanity

[31]The term "mission" was used here to refer to Protestant churches, i.e. churches that were not historically known in Ethiopia but came to the country as a result of more recent mission activity.

[32]I.e. evangelicals.

Though an answer with this level of historical and theological sophistication was clearly an exception, it does demonstrate that the historical development of Christology in the Ethiopian context has influenced at least some of the present clergy. Even in the Alert\Gebre Kristos neighborhood there are those who reject the doctrine of Christ's two natures because it is "Nestorian" and connected with Chalcedon and the Catholics.

## Two Natures

Not all subjects rejected the idea that Christ had two natures. Ten subjects responded favorably when asked how they would answer someone who suggested that Christ had two natures. Six of these ten responded as if this were the first time they had considered such an idea, but that it sounded like a good one. Four subjects responded as if they had previously considered the idea of Christ having two natures and had accepted it.

### "That's a Good Idea"

Four women and two men responded positively to the idea that Christ had two natures, while indicating that this was a new thought for them. Five of these subjects said, "That's a good idea" (*"teru hasab no"*). One quickly added, "But I'm not educated. I haven't studied that." Several others added a further explanation. One said, "He had a human nature because of his birth of Mary. He had a divine nature because he always obeyed the Father's will." Another reasoned, "He had human flesh so was human. He was divine and had God's Holy Spirit. Yes, we could say he had two natures." Two others also added that since Christ was man and God, two natures was "a good way to say it."

It may be possible to identify the factors that helped make these subjects agreeable to the idea that Christ had two natures. Five of the six were under thirty years old. Three of the women, including the only one who was over thirty, had had exposure to evangelical friends. It is possible that their age and previous exposure to new ideas contributed to these six subjects being more willing than the general population to accept the idea that Christ had two natures.

## "That's What I Believe"

Four subjects readily accepted the idea that Christ had two natures as something they had always believed. Three of these were laymen and one was a debtara. The debtara surprisingly insisted that "two natures" was what the Orthodox Church officially taught. However, this debtara had previously had extensive discussions with evangelicals, and it may be that he was expressing his thinking in terms that he thought the researcher would understand, or was attempting to gloss over a possible area of disagreement in order to please the researcher. Two of the other men had also had previous exposure to evangelicals. The only man who had had little or no exposure to evangelicals and who readily agreed that Christ had two natures was a thirty-three year old who claimed to regularly attend Gebre Kristos Church, but said he had learned little from the sermons preached there. All he knew about Christ, he said, he had learned by reading his Bible and other religious books. He responded to the initial interview question about Christ's nature by saying that he had two natures.

> Certain things happened to Christ that couldn't happen to God: he was crucified, was tired, was beaten. Certain things happened to Christ that couldn't happen to a man: he commanded others, he had authority over the world, he healed, he saved. So he had both a divine and a human nature.[33]

This man was clearly unaffected by the historical clash over the nature of Christ; furthermore, he did not think that describing Christ as having two natures would destroy the unity of his person or imply that he was less than divine or divided against himself. Though he was an exception, he demonstrates that at least some individuals in the Ethiopian Orthodox context are willing to describe Christ as having both a human and a divine nature.

### Summary: One Nature

Most subjects rejected the idea that Christ had two natures. Laypeople felt that speaking of Christ's two natures would detract from his deity or imply that he was divided against himself. Clergy agreed with these dangers, but also emphasized that one-nature Christology was what the Ethiopian

---

[33]"*Baheriy*" was the Amharic word used.

Orthodox Church believed and was a safeguard against heretically dividing Christ's person.

A minority of about twenty percent of all subjects favored the idea that Christ had two natures. These tended to be people who had had exposure to evangelicals or those who were younger and more inclined to accept new ideas. Those who accepted a two-nature Christology suggested that it was a good way to express his full deity and full humanity.

### Christ As Intercessor-Mediator

One result of the growth of evangelicalism in Ethiopia in the last quarter of the twentieth century has been fresh Christological questions which the Ethiopian Orthodox Church has had to address. Evangelicals have emphasized that there is no need for anyone to stand between God and humankind except the person of Jesus Christ, an idea that conflicts with the Orthodox emphasis on the need for many intercessor-mediators (*amalajoch*)[34] to stand between human beings and God. The evangelical emphasis on Christ as *amalaj* has raised the question among the Orthodox: Is Christ an *amalaj*? Almost all Orthodox agree that there are other *amalajoch*,[35] but the question of whether Christ is also an *amalaj* has begun to be

---

[34] See footnote 4 on pages 11 and 12 and Glossary of Amharic Terms.

[35] The only exceptions would be those who are part of the recent renewal movement in the EOC and who no longer acknowledge any *amalaj* except Christ.

debated among the Orthodox.[36] One cannot understand Orthodox perceptions on the nature of Christ without understanding Orthodox ideas about Christ as *amalaj*.

## Christ is Not an *Amalaj*

Most subjects agreed that Christ is not an *amalaj* because he himself *is* God.[37] Several subjects responded to the question "Is Christ an *amalaj*?" by answering, "To whom would he mediate or intercede? He himself is God."[38] A younger man gave a lengthily answer, explaining that God the Father, God the Son, and God the Holy Spirit are all equal in divinity, and then asked, "How could [Christ] be an *amalaj* to God? To whom would he mediate? To treat him as an *amalaj* would be to treat him as less than God." One older man was even more shocked at the suggestion that Christ could be an *amalaj* and responded, "How? To whom would he mediate, Satan?" The question almost seemed blasphemous to him, because it implied that some being could be more authoritative or more divine than Christ. A close connection clearly existed in

---

[36]See, for example, Alemayehu (1995, 43-54) who contends that Christ is an *amalaj*.

[37]Seven women, fourteen men, and all thirteen clergy agreed that Christ was not an *amalaj*.

[38]One woman, four laymen and four clergy gave answers similar to this. One man said, "He is the knower and the sender. How could he be an *amalaj*? To whom would he mediate?" A priest responded, "He is the Merciful One, not an *amalaj*."

subjects' minds between Christ's divinity and his not being an *amalaj*. A monk answered simply, "No, he is God."

## A *Temalaj*, Not an *Amalaj*

Many subjects offered alternatives to the idea that Christ is an *amalaj*. The first alternative was that he was not an *amalaj*, but a *temalaj*.[39] One older man said, "He could be either an *amalaj* or a *temalaj*. We know that he is one to whom mediation is given, so he cannot be an *amalaj*." Several subjects told stories to illustrate how the process of intercession and mediation worked. One debtara explained: "If I have a request of you, I might go through Petros (a mutual friend) to mediate for me. But I cannot be a mediator to myself. A savior cannot also be an *amalaj*."

## Christ *Was* an *Amalaj*; But No Longer

A second alternative to Christ's presently being an *amalaj* was that he *had been* an *amalaj* when he was on earth, but that he was *no longer* an *amalaj*.[40] A older layman said, "When he was a man on earth, he did the work of reconciliation. Now he is God, so how can he mediate to God?" A deacon said that Christ's

> mediatorship is finished. When he was on earth he prayed and offered requests as a mediator. For example, he told

---

[39] A *temalaj* is one who receives intercession or mediation. See the Glossary of Amharic Terms. One woman, five laymen, and three clergy referred to Christ as a *temalaj*.

[40] One layman and four clergy gave answers similar to this.

Peter he would pray for him. Now, however, he is judge and God, and the Father has given him judgment. To whom would he mediate?

A deacon quoted Isaiah 53:12[41] as proof that Christ was a mediator until he bore sin on the cross; after that he became one who receives mediation.

The feeling that Christ is not presently an *amalaj* was clearly related in subjects' minds to Christ's now being only God and no longer a man. When he was a man he was an *amalaj*; now that he is no longer a man he could no longer be an *amalaj*. A priest who had said Christ was now "the Merciful One", and so not an *amalaj*, added "he was an *amalaj* when he was on earth, but now he is only God." Another priest said, "He was an *amalaj* when he was on earth, but now he is not a man, so he is not an *amalaj*." A deacon was equally explicit, saying that Christ had been an *amalaj* when he was on earth, but "because he is not presently a man, he cannot be an *amalaj*."

## Direct Prayer to Christ

Though not widely held, a third alternative to the idea that Christ is an *amalaj* was the response that it is not necessary for Christ to be an *amalaj*, because his followers can go directly to him without passing through an *amalaj*.[42]

---

[41] ". . . For he bore the sin of many, and made intercession for the transgressors."

[42] Many subjects said that they prayed to God or Christ, but only two laymen and one debtara said that because a person could pray directly to Christ it was not necessary to

An older layman described how rich people had a guard through whom visitors had to pass before they could reach the owner of the house. "But no *amalaj* is needed for Christ," he continued, "because he himself is the door. We can come directly to him." A young widow described the effectiveness of prayer directly to Christ telling a story of how her house had been collapsing due to heavy rains. Encouraged by some evangelical friends, she prayed directly to Christ and some of her neighbors came the next day to repair it. She added that when she tells Christ, "The children you gave me are hungry," he provides food the next day. Though strongly Orthodox and somewhat suspicious of evangelicals, this woman has become convinced that prayer directly to Christ, apart from prayer through the *amalajoch*, is effective.

## Other *Amalajoch*

Subjects frequently answered the question about whether or not Christ was an *amalaj* by mentioning others they considered to be *amalajoch*. The Virgin Mary was the most common *amalaj* mentioned. The angels Gabriel and Michael and St. George were also mentioned frequently. Other *amalajoch* mentioned at least once by subjects included the apostles and Ethiopian saints such as St. Estifanos, St.

---

go through an *amalaj*. Another man added an interesting variation, saying that he could go directly to Christ and ask for forgiveness if he had sinned unintentionally, but when he sinned intentionally he had to go to Christ through the *amalajoch*.

Menfes Qedus, St. Tekle Haimanot, St. Gebre Kristos, St. Medhane Alem and the Tsadeqan.[43] One man responded that the *amalajoch* "were all over the place" ("*moltowal*"; literally "they have filled" or "they abound"). An older woman said, "There are forty-four *tabots*[44] in the Ethiopian Orthodox Church; we pray to all of them."

Subjects often explained prayer to the *amalajoch* in one of several ways.[45] First, many subjects emphasized that prayer to these other *amalajoch* was not equal to worshipful prayer to God. "We pray to the *amalajoch*, but we don't submit

---

[43] Three women and three laymen said that St. *Medhane Alem* ("Savior of the World") was a different person than Jesus Christ. In most cases they defined Medhane Alem as a strictly human saint and *amalaj* who was like any other human saint. Three women and one layman also said that the Virgin Mary was greater than Jesus Christ. Two women explained that "a mother is always greater than the one she bears."

[44] The *tabot* is the flat, rectangular wooden box which serves as a representation of the Ark of the Covenant and which consecrates an Ethiopian Orthodox church building. "*Tabot*" is often translated as "ark." Each *tabot* has the name of one of the saints of the EOC (all of whom can serve as *amalajoch*) and the *tabot* gives its name to its church. Many members of the Ethiopian Orthodox Church will commonly equate the *tabot* itself with the saint for whom it is named. When asked if there was a difference between *Medhane Alem* ("Savior of the World) and Jesus, a woman replied, "Of course, they each have their own *tabot* and each have their own [saint's] day." See the Glossary of Amharic Terms.

[45] EOC perspectives on the *amalajoch* is not the main subject of this thesis. However, many subjects clarified their answers to questions about Christ by extensively talking about the *amalajoch*. The ethnographic method being used emphasizes the importance of "thick description" of subjects' own categories in order to gain understanding, and so their answers are included here. In particular, explanations about prayer to the *amalajoch* provide valuable insight into how subjects perceived Christ.

to them or worship them" said one man. Another man emphasized that there were two kinds of worship ("*segedet*"), the kind that simply gives honor, and worship that exalts a being as God ("*amlako segedet*"). Only the former is given to the *amalajoch*, he insisted. A priest said that the *amalajoch* intercede for him because of his prayer, "but only the creator has mercy" on him. A younger woman said that "Prayer to God is different from prayer to the *amalajoch*. Prayer to the *amalajoch* is only praise." An older man said that he prayed to Christ, "but I only honor the *tabot*."[46]

Second, many subjects emphasized that prayer to the *amalajoch* was really prayer to God because they simply granted access to God or carried prayers to God. One man explained that Michael, Gabriel, and the righteous saints of old are Christ's workers, but Christ himself is the creator. The worker is always the *amalaj*, but Christ is the one to whom they take prayers. The deacon who became a *meri-gaeta* agreed that people could bring requests to the *amalajoch*, but insisted that they were not really praying to the *amalajoch* because they simply passed those prayers on to God. An older woman said, "Gebre Kristos hears my prayers and takes them to Jesus." An older layman said that "any church in Gabriel's name is God's church. Prayer in Gabriel's name is really prayer to God." A young woman similarly said that when she

---

[46]See note on page 161 and the Glossary of Amharic Terms.

was at a church with the name of an *amalaj* she honored that *amalaj* in her prayers, "but I'm really praying to Christ." A priest said, "We have to believe in [Michael and Gabriel] to come to God. Those who believe in them are expressing their belief in Christ." Several subjects illustrated the *amalajoch* as being like a guard who stands at the outside of a building or compound and carries the requests of petitioners to the owner or official. Even as the request is really to the owner or the official, but the guard carries the request, so prayer is really to God, but the *amalaj* carries the prayer to God.

Third, some subjects emphasized that God himself had delegated authority to the *amalajoch* to hear and answer the prayers of his people. "A king will delegate authority to his subjects, telling one to do this and another to do that. God delegates authority in the same way to his angels," one man said. A deacon who served as a religious teacher quoted from the Psalms.[47]

> God said, "You are gods." These are the saints. After death, they become like angels; they no longer die. And because of the good works they have done on earth, they receive this exalted position and are able to be mediators. Remember in Luke 16 about Abraham and Lazarus. When the rich man was able to talk to Abraham, though a great gulf separated them, Abraham was able to hear his prayers and pass them on. This shows that those who are dead are able to speak and to speak for us after death.

God gave the righteous saints of old and the angels the responsibility of serving as *amalajoch* after death.

---

[47]The deacon did not give the specific reference, but was referring to Psalm 82:6.

Fourth, some subjects said that praying through the *amalajoch* was no different from asking a friend to pray for them. "All of us can be *amalajoch* as we pray for others," one young layman said. A deacon referred to the death of Stephen (who prayed for his persecutors as he died), 2 Corinthians 5:18,[48] and James 5:16[49] to prove that intercession for others was acceptable, and, hence, asking the *amalajoch* to take requests to God was acceptable. Another deacon gave Job as an example of someone who prayed for his friends; the *amalajoch* could intercede in the same way Job had. A priest sought to prove that *amalajoch* who had died were spiritually alive, and so it was acceptable to ask them to take requests to God: he said that Jesus had quoted a passage where God said he was the God of Abraham, Isaac and Jacob, and that he was the God of the living and not the God of the dead.[50]

Fifth, subjects sometimes justified prayer through the *amalajoch* because they were weak and sinful and the *amalajoch* were closer to God. One woman said that there was a wall of sin between God and people, but "the *amalajoch* bring us to God." Another woman said that she was "a poor sinner," but if she went to the *amalajoch*, "God will have mercy because of

---

[48] "All this is from God, who reconciled us to himself through Christ and gave us the ministry of reconciliation."

[49] "Therefore confess your sins to each other and pray for each other so that you may be healed. The prayer of a righteous man is powerful and effective."

[50] Mark 12:26-27.

their prayers.[51] A man agreed that it was possible to pray directly to God, but that when people were deep in sin and crime, they must pray to the *amalajoch* and reconcilers, implying that the deeper a person was in sin, the more he needed an *amalaj*. A young deacon explained his need for the *amalajoch* by saying that

> they are better than me, so they can carry my requests for forgiveness. For example, you may have a friend that I can't talk to, but I may ask you to carry my request to him. In the same way, the righteous men who are better than me can carry my requests to Christ.

An older man referred to Moses, who prayed for mercy for Israel when they had sinned. "That's the way I pray to others," he said. "To ask God to withhold his anger."

Sixth, subjects occasionally said that prayer to the *amalajoch* was good because they deserved special honor. Speaking of Michael, Gabriel, St. George, and the Virgin Mary, one older man said, "They all have their own prayer books that tell us how to pray to them. We must give these holy ones honor."

Finally, a few subjects justified prayer to the *amalajoch* simply because prayer to them was effective in day-to-day needs. One woman said that

> Christ came to save the soul, but if there are real problems, especially sickness, people go to these *amalajoch* to save them. So they deserve to be honored and worshipped as divine because God has saved through them.

---

[51]This woman included as *amalajoch* living nuns who had given up their possessions and given themselves to prayer.

An older man said that "we can call on the angels, and it doesn't hurt to call on them, because they are the ones who supply solutions to our problems."

## Christ Is an *Amalaj*

Ten of the women who were interviewed felt that Christ was an *amalaj*. However, for five of these women, evidence existed that they did not understand "*amalaj*" specifically as "intercessor-mediator" but simply as an exalted title of which they felt Christ was worthy. Three of those who felt Christ was an *amalaj* said that he was only God, and was not a man. Several said that Christ was an *amalaj*, but they quickly added that they knew more about, and primarily prayed to, other *amalajoch*. Many then began to share the importance of other *amalajoch* to their lives, such as Mary or the angels Gabriel and Michael. Two women agreed that Christ was an *amalaj* but that he was higher than the "messengers" of God, like Gabriel and Michael, and so it was necessary to pray to them.

Of the men who were interviewed, the only three who said that Christ was an *amalaj* were the three who thought that he was only an exalted human being, like the other *amalajoch*, and was not divine in any sense. All three were consistent in their answer to the question, "Was Christ an *amalaj*?" All three agreed that he was "like the other *amalajoch*."

## Summary: Christ is Not an Intercessor-Mediator

Almost all subjects agreed that Christ was not presently an intercessor-mediator to God. Many explained this by saying that he was himself God--one who receives intercession--and so it was impossible for him to be one who intercedes or mediates. Some added that he *had* been an intercessor-mediator when he was on earth as a man, but since he was no longer a man, he was no longer an intercessor-mediator. A few subjects felt that Christ did not need to be an intercessor-mediator, because his followers could pray directly to him. About half of the women interviewed felt Christ was an intercessor-mediator, but most put more emphasis on other intercessor-mediators, and some showed evidence of understanding the word for "intercessor-mediator" to simply be an exalted title of which Christ was worthy. Three men consistently asserted that Christ was no more than any other human intercessor-mediator.

Subjects preferred to talk about the other intercessor-mediators in the Ethiopian Orthodox Church. Prayer to them was explained as being less than worship of God, a means of praying to God, something God himself had authorized, the same as asking a friend to pray for them, effective, and something that the holy people of old deserved.

## A Relationship With Christ

Subjects were asked about their relationship with Christ to further probe their sense of distance from or closeness to him, and to again allow them to use their own frame of reference to talk about how they understood the person of Christ. A variety of answers were given,[52] but certain clear patterns emerged about how subjects perceived their present relationship with Christ.

### A Relationship of Prayer

Women, laymen, and clergy all frequently mentioned that their primary means to have a relationship with Christ was through prayer.[53] One young women said that she had a relationship with Christ "of spirit; a meeting of spirits in prayer." An older women repeated similar words: "When I pray, God's spirit meets me in my spirit." A younger man said that Christ is only "found through prayer." A priest said the only way to have a relationship with Christ was through prayer. Most subjects characterized their prayers to Christ as times of meeting with Christ, asking for his protection, taking their daily needs to him, and humbling themselves before him.

---

[52] When asked about her relationship with Christ, one woman did not say anything about Jesus Christ, but told a story of a time when St. Gabriel had saved her from a hyena.

[53] Six women, nine laymen, and three clergy described their relationship with Christ as primarily one of prayer.

### Women: A Relationship of Love

In addition to mentioning prayer, women frequently described their relationship to Christ as one of affection, love, and closeness.[54] Three women said they had a "father-daughter" relationship with Christ, and another said that her relationship with Christ was "better than with a parent." Two others said their relationship was one of love. One women said literally, "I have much relationship with Christ,"[55] implying frequency and intimacy in her relationship with Christ. Another said, "I love him. Whenever I have a concern, I take it to him."

Laymen and clergy were much less likely to describe their relationship with Christ as one of love or closeness. One man mentioned that Christ was kind to him, and two clergy mentioned that Christ was their savior from sin and the devil.

### Laymen and Clergy: A Relationship of Distance and Submission

Laymen and clergy were far more likely to describe their relationship with Christ as one of distance, submission,

---

[54] There was no clear correlation between women who said that Christ was an intercessor-mediator and those who described their relationship with Christ in terms of love and closeness. Some women who said Christ was *not* an intercessor-mediator described their relationship with him as one of love and closeness and some women who said that Christ *was* an intercessor-mediator said nothing about love or closeness when describing their relationship with Christ.

[55] Amharic: "*Bezu genunyenet allegn.*"

and servanthood.[56] Five men and two clergy said something about their distance from Christ or the difficulty in having a relationship with Christ. One older man asked, "He's my master (*balebeit*). How can I know about him? How can I know him? I come to him in humble, submissive, 'flat-on-my-face' prayer."[57] Another older man said, "I have to beg for mercy before him. I'm not like one of these angels. How can a man who is clothed in flesh have a relationship with the creator?"

Three men said they had no relationship with Christ, two of them adding that they hoped to have a relationship with him after they died. Four men explained their relationship with Christ as one of obedience. One said that he was Christ's "servant", and so he must fast in order to receive forgiveness. Another mentioned that because God was his creator and he was a sinner, he must fast and otherwise mortify his flesh to have any relationship with God. Four men described their relationship to Christ as creature to creator.

Clergy also described their relationship with Christ as one of distance and submission. One monk said that he was "a weak slave" of Christ. The deacon who became a *meri-gaeta* said that Christ was "distant, he's far from me because I'm a sinner. Christ has no falseness in him, and so I am very far

---

[56] One woman mentioned obedience to Christ's commands as descriptive of her relationship with him; one woman described herself as Christ's "servant;" one woman described Christ as her creator; one woman described Christ as her sovereign (*chay*).

[57] Amharic: *Meseged*

from Christ." Six clergy mentioned obedience as the essence of their relationship with Christ. One said, "If I obey his commands, I have a relationship with him. My relationship is based on my obedience. If I obey his commands, I will inherit the kingdom of God." Another said that his obedience to Christ was necessary for him to receive eternal life.

### Clergy: A Relationship Through the Eucharist

Though not frequently mentioned, some clergy described their relationship with Christ by talking about the holy communion, or eucharist. One deacon said that the way to have a relationship with Christ was to pray, do good works, and "take Christ's flesh and blood," and he quoted John 6:54[58] to support his reasoning. A priest made a reference to the eucharist in a subtle word play, saying that he had a relationship with Christ because Christ took on flesh, and his "flesh was broken" for him, quoting Christ's words at the last supper.

### A Relationship of Faith

A few subjects mentioned faith as the key to their relationship with Christ.[59] Most added very little except to say, "I have a relationship of faith with Christ." One man who had expressed Christ's distance from him because he is

---

[58] "Whoever eats my flesh and drinks my blood remains in me and I in him."

[59] Two women, two laymen, and one deacon.

creator added that a person could still have a relationship with him "by faith;" he then added that he meant "faithful obedience, our clean lives." Another said that he had a "relationship of faith" which had brought him away from sin. A deacon said that his relationship with Christ was "full of faith," adding that he was trusting God for his daily food and for protection from the devil. Those subjects which described their relationship with Christ as one of faith seemed to mean they prayed to Christ and obeyed him.

### Summary: Popular Perspectives on the Nature of Christ Among Ethiopian Orthodox in Alert/Gebre Kristos, Addis Ababa

Most Ethiopian Orthodox in the Alert/Gebre Kristos neighborhood of Addis Ababa believed that Jesus Christ was both God and man when he walked the earth. He was God clothed in flesh, a perfect *tewahedo* ("union") of divinity and humanity. However, many believed that his humanity was somewhat different from that of other people; his was not a common humanity. After his resurrection and ascension Christ left his humanity and was only divine.

Most Ethiopian Orthodox in the Alert/Gebre Kristos neighborhood strongly maintained that Christ had only one nature. They believed that to suggest that he had two natures threatened his deity, suggested that his mind was divided against itself, and threatened the unity of his divinity and humanity. Most agreed that Christ is not now an intercessor-mediator, though he may have been. One reason why he is not now an intercessor-mediator is because he is no longer a man.

Ethiopian Orthodox in Alert/Gebre Kristos felt they had a relationship with Christ through prayer. Many women felt love and closeness to him; many men felt they have a relationship of submission and distance.

What is the relevance of these findings to ministry in the Alert/Gebre Kristos neighborhood? Before conclusions may be drawn, a theological framework for evaluating these findings must be established.

# CHAPTER 6

## FRAMEWORK FOR THEOLOGICAL AND MISSIOLOGICAL REFLECTION

Before historical, official, linguistic, and popular perceptions of the on the nature of Christ in the Ethiopian Orthodox Church can be evaluated, a theological framework from which they can be analyzed must be established. Two parts to this framework are necessary. First, the contextual nature of theology must be defined. Second, a Christology against which the Orthodox Church's Christology can be compared must be stated.

### Theology in Context

The Orthodox Church's perspective on the nature of Christ cannot be evaluated until the contextual nature of theology is defined. The approach for doing contextual theology adopted in this thesis is *biblically-centered contextual theologizing*, similar to what Schreiter and Bevans call a "translation model" (Schreiter 1985, 6; Bevans 1985, 189). The thinking of theologians who work within the translation model will provide the framework for evaluating perspectives on the nature of Christ in the EOC. Biblically-centered contextual theology maintains the distinction between "the 'textuality' of the Christian faith and the 'contextuality' of the church and our particular understanding of the faith" (Stackhouse 1988, 6). It assumes that there is a transcontextual faith which can be transmitted to all cultures. The biblically-centered model for contextual theologizing will be explained in two ways: by contrasting it with exegesis and context-centered models for theologizing and by defining its essential characteristics.

### Exegesis-Centered and Context-Centered Models for Theologizing

Biblically-centered contextual theologizing is based on a hermeneutic which stands between an exegesis-centered model and a context-centered model for theologizing.

#### Exegesis-Centered Theologizing

In his discussion of how much theology is "inevitably influenced by the ideological, cultural, and socio-political values and commitments of the interpreter," Conn identifies the exegesis-centered model as the traditional evangelical model of hermeneutics. This approach defines exegesis "narrowly in terms of the language of the text," tends to isolate words from their cultural context and assumes they can thus be easily translated into another language, and views truth and practice as distinct and separate steps in theologizing (Conn 1983, 40-41).

The exegesis-centered model for theologizing is represented by Larkin who believes that interpreters can and should divorce themselves as much as possible from their own context in order to understand the meaning of the text as it was intended to be understood by the original author.

> One's cultural preunderstanding can often control one's exegesis so that what is perceived as the meaning of a text is really foisted on it by the contemporary context. However, interpreters who consciously set aside their cultural preunderstanding can be confident that the grammatical-historical-literary context will enable them to find the plain and definite meaning of the text. (Larkin 1988, 301)

Larkin separates the cultural context of the interpreter from the process of interpretation in several other ways. First, he draws a clear distinction between meaning as found in the cultural context and meaning as found in the author's intent. Second, he believes that "it is important to view interpretation as separate from application" (Larkin 1988, 313). "The Bible makes a distinction between the meaning and significance of a text and finds the locus of meaning in the author's intended sense rather than in his context" (Larkin 1988, 313; c.f. 243). Third, he is uncomfortable with the idea of interpreters bringing their questions and concerns to the text, fearful that this will distort their understanding of what the text itself is saying (Larkin 1988, 298; 306; 309). Fourth, he postulates a "horizon of truth" which stands beyond the horizons of the text and interpreter and which "makes the [interpretation] process possible" (Larkin 1988, 310; c.f. 219). Finally, he gives inadequate attention to the degree to which the context of interpreters may shape their understanding of the text.

The exegesis-centered model for theologizing properly recognizes the central role of understanding the Scriptures in their original context if theology is to retain divine authority. Many of Larkin's ideas have merit and deserve careful consideration. However, he does not give adequate attention to either the context in which the Bible was first written or the context of the interpreter. Because Scripture was written in a cultural-historical context, and because it is always read in a cultural-historical context, context can never be divorced from the process of hermeneutics and theologizing. The exegesis-centered model is ultimately inadequate because it does not give enough attention to the role of context in the process of theologizing.

## Context-Centered Theologizing

In sharp contrast to Larkin's position is the approach of theologians who see the interpreter's context as being a *primary* source of data for theologizing. Many of these theologians tend toward "contextualism," the belief that "everything of basic significance grows out of the contextual experience" of those who are theologizing (Stackhouse 1988, 8).

Muzorewa (1985) is a good example of a context-centered theologian. Speaking of theologizing in the African context, he lists the Bible as *a* primary source, but gives equal priority to African traditional religions, African independent churches, and the All-Africa Conference of

Churches. Dickson (1984) likewise gives equal weight to the Scripture, African culture, personal experience, and church tradition as sources for theology. These context-centered sources of theology play a major role in the way the context-centered theologian understands the Scriptures. Context becomes equal or greater to Scripture as a source of theology. It is the controlling factor in theologizing.

One example of context-centered theology is Sawyerr's suggestion that the Church would be best understood in Africa as "the Great Family," and that with this understanding of the Church, ancestors could "be readily embraced within the framework of the universal church and be included within the communion of the saints" (Sawyerr 1968, 94). By using context as the primary, controlling source of theology, Sawyerr has developed a theology primarily centered in African culture rather than in the Scriptures.

Context-centered theologizing properly recognizes that *all* theologizing will be affected by the context of the theologian. However, context-centered approaches are also inadequate because their emphasis on context as the primary source of theology replaces the Scriptures as the normative basis for theology, removing any absolute foundation for theology.

## Biblically-Centered Contextual Theologizing

Standing between Larkin and Sawyerr, Dickson, and Muzorewa are evangelical theologians such as Tienou, Padilla, Conn, and, to some extent, Kraft. These men make the Scriptures the primary source of theology, but they also recognize the significant role of the context in theologizing. Their thinking might be called "biblically-centered contextual theology." Biblically-centered contextual theology recognizes both the priority of the biblical paradigm in theologizing and the contextual nature of theology.

### The Contextual Nature of Theology

Biblically-centered contextual theology begins with the understanding that all theology is contextual. Only the Word of God itself is absolute for all times and cultures. Theology is the reflection of the community of Christian believers on God through his revelation of himself, primarily in the Scriptures, in light of the ever-changing human context. In an essay on the future of African theology, Sundkler defines theology as

> an ever-renewed re-interpretation to new generations and peoples of the given Gospel, a representation of the will and way of the one Christ in a dialogue with new thought-forms and cultural patterns. (Sundkler 1960, 493)

In more recent studies, evangelicals have expressed similar thoughts. Padilla asserts that

> theology includes but is far more than exegesis. It is the result of a process of transposing the Word of God from its original Hebrew or Graeco-Roman *milieu* into a

contemporary situation, for the purpose of producing in the modern readers or hearers the same kind of impact that the original message was meant to produce in its original historical context. (Padilla 1983, 79)

Since theology is not itself the Word of God, but the reflection of God's people on God's Word in light of their ever-changing cultures and circumstances, then theology has a close relationship to context. "There is no theology that is not a contextual theology" (Gilliland 1989, 12; c.f. Hundley 1993; Kraft 1979, 291).

The contextual nature of theology is rooted in the contextual nature of all understanding. Anthony Thiselton has clearly demonstrated that Scripture is always understood in a personal, historical, and cultural context. There is no "a-cultural" interpretation of Scripture. Because interpreters are always influenced by their contexts, interpretation is not a matter of a "subject" standing apart from, observing, and objectively interpreting an "object;" rather interpretation is always an interactive process between the interpreter and the text.

> It is simply philosophically naive to imply that some interpreters can have access to self-evidently "true" meanings as over against their interpretation of it . . . . The notion of the hermeneutical circle[1] is not, then, a sell-out to man-centered relativism, but a way of describing the process of understanding in the interpretation of a text." (Thiselton 1977b, 327)

---

[1] Thiselton often speak of the "hermeneutical circle," but his use of the term brings him close to Grant Osborne's concept of The hermeneutical spiral (1991). The concept of the spiral is preferred because it implies progressive movement toward understanding the text, a concept which Thiselton endorses (see below pages 184-186).

Because "*the modern interpreter, no less than the text, stands in a given historical context and tradition,*" the interpreter's understanding of the text, and the theology developed from that understanding, will always be historically and culturally conditioned (Thiselton 1980, 11; italics original). The language, culture, historically-conditioned theology, personal circumstances, and questions of interpreters will all shape the way they understand the text (Thiselton 1980, 166; 309; 311-12; 315; 360; 374-75). Theology is never equal to God's revelation, but will always be a personal, historical and cultural reflection on God's revelation.

## The Priority of the Biblical Paradigm

Theology will always be framed in the context of the theologian, but it must never be *merely* a reflection of context. Even though biblically-centered contextual theology recognizes that all theology is contextual, it insists on the priority of the Biblical paradigm in the process of theologizing.

The Bible claims to be a unique revelation from God which was given in a particular historical setting, but which continues to speak to people in every time and every culture (2 Timothy 3:16-17; 2 Peter 1:21; c.f. frequent quotes of the Old Testament in the New Testament). It claims to be more than a model of on-going revelation; it is itself the primary tool of God's revealing himself to humankind. Therefore, regardless of the theologian's culture or historical context, theologizing must begin by seeking the meaning of the text in its original context. The interpreters'

> task is to let the text speak, whether they agree with it or not, and this demands that they understand what the text meant in its original situation . . . . No interpreters, regardless of their culture, are free to make the text say whatever they want it to say. (Padilla 1980, 71)

Kraft agrees that interpreters "must engage in exegesis to discover what the original utterances meant to those whose interpretational reflexes were the same as those of the authors" (Kraft 1979, 133).

Tite Tienou reflects the priority of the biblical text and the clear distinction between biblically-centered contextual theology and merely context-centered theology when he examines the proposals of Sawyerr, Fasholé-Luke, and Haselbarth that the Church should be viewed as the Great Family of God and that non-Christian ancestors will be included in God's communion of the saints. He criticizes these scholars for practicing "mnemic hermeneutics," which is

> allowing one's own natural analogy to become the crucial key in understanding Scripture. In this case, the African understanding of family as composed of the living, the dead and the unborn is read back into Scripture without prior questioning. This in turn makes the biblical message go beyond its intended meaning. (Tienou 1984, 160)

Tienou strongly affirms that interpreters must "let the biblical paradigm control" their interpretation and warns that emphasizing "the African context more than the biblical paradigm" will lead to a "distortion of the biblical message" (Tienou 1984, 159).

Speaking of the priority of the biblical paradigm is similar to saying that the first goal of the interpreter should be to seek the "authorial intent" (Hirsch 1967) of the writer.[2] The first goal of theologizing must be to read the text the way it was meant to be read. If theology is a reflection on God's revelation, especially in his Word, then theologians must make the starting point of their theology the priority of the biblical paradigm by seeking to understand the message of Scripture in its original historical-cultural context. Theologians and interpreters should use all of the tools of history, linguistics, and the social sciences to accomplish this (Kraft 1979, 131-39).

Some theologians have followed the lead of philosophers such as Gadamer, Wittgenstein, and Heidegger and

---

[2] It is beyond the scope of this thesis to discuss in detail the strengths and weaknesses of Hirsch's concept of "authorial intent" which have been clearly identified by Osborne (1991, 393-94), Erickson (1993, 11-32), and Thiselton. Thiselton correctly concludes regarding Hirsch that: (1) he does not fall into the "intentional fallacy" (Thiselton 1992, 59), (2) his concerns that there must be some criteria "which will allow us to determine when some 'mistake' or misunderstanding has occurred" are valid (Thiselton 1992, 13), but (3) "it only postpones rather than solves the problem if we follow Hirsch in restricting 'meaning' to a largely *semantic* notion of meaning" (Thiselton 1993, 13). Thiselton's concern that seeking the "authorial intent" is an inadequate reading strategy for certain kinds of biblical texts, however, does not seem as valid. He endorses the concept of seeking to read all texts the way "authorial agents" meant them to be read (Thiselton 1990, 290); this is the essence of "authorial intent."

speculated that the preunderstanding of interpreters so shapes their minds that they will never be able to understand the message of the text itself. Croatto exemplifies such theologians, claiming that "exegesis is eisegesis, and anybody who claims to be doing only the former is, wittingly or unwittingly, engaged in subterfuge" (Croatto 1981, 2). Croatto believes that all theologians are so strongly influenced by their preunderstanding and context that it is impossible to read the text the way it was meant to be read.

However, Thiselton has responded to the philosophy of doubt in interpretation by pointing out that it is possible for interpreters and theologians to extend their own horizons in the direction of the horizon of the text. Readers of Scripture are not doomed to simply confirm what they already know and believe.

> We approach questions of knowledge, or we seek to understand, from within horizons already bounded by our finite situatedness within the flow of history. But it is possible for these finite and historically conditioned horizons to be enlarged, and to expand. In actualizations of understanding or encounter between readers and texts, the boundaries of horizons may be extended and moved, and thus come to constitute *new* horizons . . . . Is this not . . . one of the most fundamental functions which biblical texts can perform? (Thiselton 1992, 6)

Thiselton suggests that the nature of historical and literary study, the nature of learning and of language, the fact that people do change their minds in spite of opposition, and revised understanding which comes through the "hermeneutical circle" are all proof that interpreters can adequately read Scriptural texts the way they were intended to be read

(Thiselton 1980, 60; 314; 380; 391; 396; 398; 1977b, 316; 1992, 34; 589.)[3]

But Thiselton not only demonstrates that it is *possible* for horizons to be extended; the task of biblical hermeneutics *demands* that horizons be extended in the direction of the text. Biblical texts claim to be interpersonal communication--revelation from God to human beings--offering "*external norms of judgement over against their readers*" (1992, 473; italics original). Interpreters and theologians are not free to allow their own context to completely shape their understanding of the text, but must seek to understand the revelatory message being communicated. For theology to be *Christian* theology, the horizons of the theologian *must* be extended in the direction of the horizon of the biblical text.

In particular, interpreters must not be too quick to dismiss the propositions of biblical writers as merely the "cultural scaffolding" of their thought.

> Was the "scaffolding" of the thoughts of the New Testament writers *only cultural*-relative, or was it also due to the

---

[3]See also Kraft (1978, 84-88; 133; 145-146), Larkin (1988, 300-312) and Osborne (1991, 366-415) for demonstrations of the possibility of adequately reading a text the way it was meant to be read. To extend one's horizons in the direction of the text, Thiselton warns against "a premature fusion of horizons which fails to preserve any tension between the past and the present" (1980, 319). To read the text the way it was meant to be read, theologians and interpreters must first "distance" themselves from the horizon of the text (1980, 326; 1992, 8) by identifying their own pre-understandings, particularly the "tensions" between their horizons and those of the text (1977b, 317).

> theological convictions which constitute part of the distinctive Hebrew-Christian tradition of thought? Was it because of cultural patterns or theological patterns that the incarnation, for example was conceived of as something unique? (1980, 74; italics original)

Many biblical concepts are not only culturally conditioned, but also *theologically* conditioned, central to the Christian paradigm. If the ideas of these texts are simply dismissed as "cultural scaffolding," then the theology that emerges will be something less than Christian. Theologizing must begin with the biblical paradigm in establishing the patterns of truth to be contextualized.

## Shared Understanding Across Contexts

An important corollary to placing priority on the biblical paradigm is that, despite contextual differences, interpreters and theologians can arrive at essentially shared meaning of biblical texts. God has communicated the truth of his word in such a way that interpreters in every culture can have "adequate, though nonabsolute, understanding of supracultural truth" (Kraft 1978, 129). Their "apprehension or expression of absolute truth is of course incomplete and partial, but that does not make such apprehension or expression relative" (Larkin 1988, 241). Interpreters will understand the text in slightly different ways because of their individual contexts and their preunderstanding, but, by placing priority on the biblical paradigm, each interpreter can also understand the text adequately.

Hirsch presents a model of understanding that shows how interpreters can understand differently but not disparately. He speaks of the meaning of a message as a "willed type." It is possible for two interpreters to notice or emphasize different specific "traits" (i.e. implications) of that type while both still correctly understand the "intrinsic genre" or meaning of the whole (Hirsch 1967, 86). "Their mutual compatibility is not based on their incompleteness or partiality, but quite the contrary on the identity of the whole meaning to which they refer" (Hirsch 1967, 132). Applied to biblical hermeneutics, interpreters from different cultures may observe different traits of individual passages of Scripture, but as long as they share the same intrinsic genre of that passage, they have adequately understood its essential meaning.[4]

An intrinsic genre may be shared by peoples across culture and history because of the essential commonality of human beings. People of all times and places are alike

---

[4]Clifford Geertz demonstrates how, even though it is impossible for a person from one culture to climb inside the mind of a person from another culture, by analyzing what the symbolic forms of a culture actually mean to the people themselves, it is possible "to produce an interpretation of the way a people lives which is neither imprisoned within their mental horizons . . . nor systematically deaf to the distinctive tonalities of their existence" (Geertz 1983, 57). In the same way that individuals can adequately understand other cultures by carefully observing their symbolic "art texts" and then relating those symbols to what they know in general about the culture, so theologians can come to understand the essential message of Scripture by carefully observing the details of a text and fitting those into the broader context.

biologically, psychologically, spiritually, and, to a large degree, socio-culturally (Kraft 1979, 84-88). All human beings also seem to share a universal frame of conceptual reference, including semantic relationships, which allow communication among peoples of different times and cultures (Hesselgrave and Rommen 1989, 161-65; Thiselton 1977a, 87). Human beings also share common life experiences--such as jokes, pain, remorse, sincerity, lying, reflecting on the past--with people from every other culture (Thiselton 1992, 249; 541-43). The work of anthropologists demonstrates both a basic unity among human beings and that people of different cultures can understand one another (Geertz 1973, 14; 35-36; 1983, 41-48; 56-57). Scripture itself seems to assume that God has authored his Word so that people from every culture can understand its "intrinsic genre."[5] Some cultures will understand certain traits, and other cultures will understand other traits. Only God, the author of Scripture, will understand all of the traits of each "willed type," or message in Scripture. But because of the commonalities of humankind around the world, all can understand the essential message of Scripture.

---

[5]For example, one of the major themes of Luke-Acts is that a message originally directed primarily to the Jews now demands a response from all people (Acts 17:30; see Strauss 1980).

## Context Affects Awareness of Aspects of the Text

Even though interpreters and theologians from different times and places can understand the same essential message of Scripture, their particular cultural, historical, and personal contexts will give them an increased awareness and sensitivity to certain details in the text. "Every culture possesses positive elements, favorable to the understanding of the Gospel" (Padilla 1980, 65). The world view, values, and images of each culture will help them see things in the Scripture that other cultures may miss. Speaking of Africa, Sundkler says,

> In the theological encounter in Africa there are certain aspects of the Biblical message which tend to carry a particular emphasis, and which take on overtones that are partially lacking in other Churches. (Sundkler 1960, 494)

On the other hand "in all cultures there are elements which conspire against the understanding of God's Word" (Padilla 1980, 65). That is, interpreters in every culture will overlook some of the traits of a text because of their context. They will be dulled and blinded by some aspects of their cultural, historical, and personal context and will consequently not see certain details of the text. Consciously and unconsciously they will excuse themselves from some of the teachings of Scripture.

> It is, of course, correct to note that human commonality makes parallels inevitable between the Bible and other religious traditions . . . . Nevertheless the differences should not be overlooked. Proper hermeneutics must wrestle with *both* parallels *and* differences. This will allow the Word of God to have a corrective function as

well as being grafted onto sound points of contact. (Tienou 1984, 161)

It is at these very points where the Word of God needs to have "a corrective function" in a culture that the theologian must be bold and proclaim the offense of the cross. As Conn points out, contextualized theology "must always insist on that particular element of Christianity that stands in direct conflict with the nonbeliever's mindset" (Conn 1984, 240).

## Context Shapes the Form Theology Takes

Even though they are seeking to read Scripture the way it was originally meant to be read, theologians are still influenced by their own cultural, historical, and personal contexts when they read Scripture. "There is no such thing as a presuppositionless theology" (Tienou 1983, 89). People do not understand until they have conceptualized something in their own minds in terms of images, experiences, and information that are already there. Understanding of the intrinsic genre of Scripture will always come through forms and symbols with which people are already familiar. "Every interpretation of the text implies a world-and-life view" (Padilla 1980, 70). Conn agrees, pointing out that theology is grounded in worldview. Worldviews "provide us with religious paradigms for 'seeing' things, pre-answers that shape our questions" (Conn 1984, 16). Even as they are attempting to read a text as it was originally meant to be read, interpreters will understand that text in terms of what they already know and have experienced.

In the same way that theologians will always conceptualize theology in forms with which they are already familiar, they will also express it in forms familiar to the people with whom the theologian is communicating. Theology will always be shaped by and expressed in the thought categories of the theologian's context.

> True theology is the attempt on the part of the church to explain and interpret the meaning of the gospel for its own life and to answer questions raised by the Christian faith, using the thought, values and categories of truth which are authentic to that place and time. (Gilliland 1989, 10-11)

One example of expressing theology in the thought categories of the context can be found in the "redemptive analogies" that Richardson (1984) has collected. For Richardson, these are indications that a residue of revelation exists in many cultures through which the gospel can be communicated. However, redemptive analogies can also be seen as cultural forms which shape the way people conceptualize theological truth and which can be used to communicate biblical theology. Because people only understand when they have conceptualized in their own thought categories, biblically-centered contextual theologians must seek to understand and express the truths of Scripture using forms which communicate within their context.

## The Relationship of Form and Meaning in the Process of Theologizing

If theology is understood and expressed in unique categories which are authentic to each culture, does that mean that the forms with which theological truth is communicated are irrelevant? Are forms always one with meanings and indispensable to accurate communication? Or are forms completely discardable, neutral vehicles to transport meaning? Are theologians free to discard the forms of Scriptures and the historical church creeds in order to express the same meaning in their own culture? How are forms related to meaning in cross-cultural communication?

Hiebert (1989) presents a balanced model of the relationship of form and meaning in communication. He points out that radically divorcing form and meaning reflects too simple a view of culture, does not take seriously the fact that symbols are created and controlled by social groups, does not reflect the long history of words and other symbols which connect form and meaning, reflects an individualistic view of human experience, and introduces a degree of relativism and pragmatism that may threaten the absolute nature of the Gospel. Instead of either identifying form and meaning or denying any intrinsic relationship between form and meaning, Hiebert suggests that the relationship between form and meaning be viewed as a continuum. Form and meaning may be arbitrarily linked, loosely linked, tightly linked, or equal.

Hiebert's model has many implications for a hermeneutic of theologizing, particularly when comparing the theological statements of theologians in two different cultures or from two different times. While they do not have the freedom to completely ignore the forms that they are using to express their understanding of the Scripture, neither should they slavishly insist on using the same exact form to express the same theological truth. Interpreters are not free to thoughtlessly impose or discard biblical forms in their theologizing. There will be some forms in Scripture that are closely tied to meaning, and therefore should be maintained transculturally.

On the other hand, forms established by churches of one culture and period of history should not be considered the only way that Christians in another time and culture can express the same theological truth. Creeds and theological formulas are expressions of biblical truth for specific times and places. As such, they unite the universal church around a common history and serve as an example of theology that was both biblical and relevant in the past. But, though they may be useful across times and cultures, none should be *imposed* transculturally (Conn 1984, 241-246).

## Contextual Theology and Inter-Cultural Theology

Because no culture can understand all of the traits of Scripture, and because each culture contains elements that will help it understand what another culture might overlook, intercultural theologizing is essential for the universal church. "Intercultural theologizing" is the sharing of local theologies developed in each cultural and historical context with churches from other contexts.

Intercultural theologizing plays at least two key roles in the process of doing theology. First, such sharing of theologies enriches the theology of the church in each context and the theology of the universal church. In particular, by listening to theologies from other contexts, theologians help preserve the priority of the biblical paradigm over their own theological presuppositions. Thiselton maintains that such a metacritical hermeneutic that practices a certain amount of suspicion towards one's own theology is an important tool in expanding one's horizons in the direction of the text. Quoting Torrence, he remarks that

> the point *where we feel ourselves under attack from the Scripture*, where our natural reason is offended by it, and where we are flung into tumults, is *the very point where genuine interpretation can take place and profound understanding be reached.* (1992, 193; italics original)

If horizons are to expand in the direction of the text, interpreters must give the most careful consideration to those interpretations of texts which most deeply offend them and disturb their broader theological system. Such disturbing interpretations of the text come through intercultural theologizing.

The second key role intercultural theologizing plays is ensuring that each contextual local theology will remain congruent with the theology of the church universal, and so remain authentically Christian (Conn 1984, 246-57). Theologies developed in each context will be expressed using different cultural forms and modes of expression, but when they becomes disparate from the cross-cultural theology of the church universal--universal in time and universal in location --they are no longer Christian theologies

Intercultural theologizing should take place at four levels: between churches of different cultures, between individuals of different educational and social levels within the churches of each culture, between different denominations and theological traditions, and between the church of each generation and the church of past generations.

Between Churches of Different Cultures

Because the church in each culture will have some areas of special insight into Scriptural truth and other areas of blindness to Scriptural truth, churches in each culture must share the fruits of their theological activity with each other. "Any monocultural perspective on truth is no more complete than the single perspective of any given individual" (Kraft 1979, 292). Believers from each culture can learn much about God by listening to the insights of their brothers and sisters from other cultures.

> There is a need for continual *cross*-fertilization and *mutual* correction; and I expect that a genuinely Asian or African theology will develop insights unavailable to unaided western theology, but which can in varying degrees be communicated to westerners to their spiritual enrichment. (Taber 1978, 10; c.f. Sundkler 1960, 510; Kraft 1979, 295).

The Gospel and its ramifications are far bigger than any one culture. There is no regional church that has a monopoly on theological truth, nor any church which has nothing to contribute to the rest of the worldwide church.

The importance of intercultural theologizing has generally been ignored by the Western church. Many in the Western church have reflected a paternalistic attitude that their theology is "objective" and uninfluenced by Western culture. Consequently, they believe, non-Western theologians should simply accept theologies worked out in the West or that, at most, fresh non-Western theologies should be adaptations of the "objective" theology Westerners have already done.[6]

But Western theologians need to realize that their theology has also been contextually conditioned. They, too, have blind spots which can be illuminated by the theology of non-Westerners. Not only must non-Western churches be free to develop biblically-centered contextual theologies that speak directly to their own situations; Western churches must listen

---

[6]Conn sees the feeling among Western theologians that their theology is "objective" and others are contextualized versions of Western theology as a major reason why much of Western theology has lost its evangelistic, missionary purpose and become more theoretical and esoteric (Conn 1984, 222-23).

to these non-Western theologies to enrich their own theologies and the cross-cultural theology of the universal church.

> Every individual, group, discipline, and culture has much to offer the rest by way of insight and specialized understanding . . . . *Theologizing by those of nonwestern cultures (if within scriptural limits) can both enrich the rest of us and alert us to deficiencies in our commonly held interpretations.* (Kraft 1979, 298; 304; italics original; c.f. 303)

Believers from every nation can enhance their understanding of God's revelation and correct their own blind spots by listening to the theology of churches from other cultures. "Every church must learn to be both learner and teacher in theologizing" (Conn 1984, 252).

Between Different Socio-Educational Levels

Not only must theologizing be done by the church in every culture; it must also be done by Christians at every social and educational level. Theology "has all too frequently been conceived as an academic discipline in which only a few intellectually qualified experts, who may or may not participate in the life of the church, are able to engage" (Padilla 1983, 81). But "reflection on truth is not an exercise of the trained elite alone" (Gilliland 1989, 26; see also Thiselton 1992, 532).

Non-professional theologians must play an especially important part in raising the questions which need to be addressed from Scripture, but they should also be part of the process of reflecting on what the Scripture says to these issues. Even as believers from different cultures will see different aspects of biblical truth, so believers from different educational and social environments within the same culture will have different but complementary insights into how the Bible is speaking to a particular issue. Professional theologians bring to the theologizing process exegetical tools and background into the historical development of theology. But theologizing is the privilege of every member of the body of Christ. It is a process which must always be done in the broad community which is living out the theology.

Between Different Theological Traditions

One of the most important forms of intercultural theologizing is the sharing of theologies between different denominations and churches of different theological traditions. Each denomination and theological tradition has a tendency to allow its theology to become a paradigm which controls the exegesis of biblical texts.

> Mere *interpretations* of texts can themselves take on the status of controlling paradigms in our lives, which, when they become both all-powerfully directive and unchallengedably 'for-ever fixed' begin to assume a quasi-idolatrous role, as securities in which we place *absolute* trust. (Thiselton 1992, 124; italics original; see also 379)

When theology begins to control exegesis, the priority of the biblical text has been lost.

To prevent theological tradition from controlling exegesis, Thiselton calls for a measure of "socio-critical *suspicion*" towards one's own theology and a willingness to listen to those from outside of one's reading community. Such socio-critical suspicion can bring about "re-valuations" and "retrieval" of textual meaning and open the possibility of renewal and change within a theological tradition (1992, 344). Theologians of every theological persuasion and every cultural group need to listen to one another, to consider how other groups interpret the text and to ask what can be learned from them.

## With the Church of Past Generations

Part of the contextual nature of all theology is its historical context. "All expressions of Christian doctrine are rooted in history and are, therefore, historically and culturally conditioned" (Muller 1991, 91). The doctrinal struggles of past generations took place in a historical context, and the creeds and confessions that emerged from those struggles were shaped by that context.

> Creeds, as an expression of the confessional character of all theologizing, are "historically situational." They are human acts of confession of God's unchanging good news, addressed to specific human cultural settings. (Conn 1984, 242)

The creeds and confessions of the church are, therefore, historical and cultural theologies addressed to particular situations the church has faced. But they also reflect a desire to reach beyond the contextual and find universal truth which will unite and provide identity for the church across generations and cultures.

> In the dialogue between the contextual and the universal, the fallible church *points beyond itself and its own context* to that which lies beyond it, especially to the

> divine promise of the future, and the universals of the cross and the resurrection . . . . Life-world interacts with system, in a way which promotes both stable identity and historical movement. (Thiselton 1992, 592)

Distinctively *Christian* theology asserts that there is universal truth. God has revealed this truth, partially in the Scriptures. Though theologies are all contextual, they are also an attempt to reach beyond what is merely situational and reflect God's universal truth. Though

> understanding of "present situations" are always interactive understandings, *always on the move* . . . *in principle* the present is to be understood as a sub-form of life to be contextualized within the *larger or "higher"* frame or form of life, shared by the interpreter, that transcends *both* horizons of particularity. (Thiselton 1992, 608; italics original)

Theology is contextual, but it is also an attempt to reflect truth that is universal. The creeds of the church are contextual attempts to do just that.

The nature of creeds as both contextual and universal theologies demands that the church neither ignore them nor unthinkingly parrot them.

> Contemporary systematic theology, therefore, cannot afford simply to repeat the language that it has been given--nor can it afford to ignore the past and attempt to strike out in new and innovative directions and expect to achieve any results or lasting significance. (Muller 1991, 94)

Because of the contextual nature of creeds, to simply repeat them is decidedly *not* to understand them or be faithful to them. Faithfulness to the contextual *and* universal nature of creeds will demand, first, carefully studying the context in which they were written, second, isolating the universal truth the creeds were seeking to express, and third, restating the truths in language which carries the same meaning in the theologians' own unique context.

> Faithfulness to such doctrines does not necessarily mean repeating them; rather it requires, in the making of any new formulations, adherence to the same directives that were involved in their first formulation. (Lindbeck 1984, 81)

Contextual theologians in the present must study and use the creeds of the past, not in slavish repetition of their words and phrases to maintain the pretention of doctrinal purity, but as past models of contextual theology. Reference to the contextual theologies of the past is a form of inter-cultural theologizing which provides today's church with a etic perspective on its own theology (Conn 1984, 204).

## Context Raises Questions for Theologizing

One of the most important roles context plays in the theologizing process is raising questions and issues for which a theology is needed. "The historical situation also contributes to the interpretive process by posing questions which demand scriptural answers" (Padilla 1980, 69). One criticism often leveled at theological education is that students learn the answers to questions that were asked hundreds of years ago, but which no one is asking today. But those great statements of faith were not forged in a contextual vacuum; they were developed throughout church history in response to pressing issues that the church was facing. Christianity is often accused of being irrelevant in non-Western contexts because it has not addressed the primary concerns of these cultures. "Theology, especially when it is truly dynamic and valid, is bound to be culturally conditioned in the questions it raises and answers" (Taber 1978, 5). Tienou encourages interpreters "to take a major problem of human existence and examine it in biblical perspective, then in a specific cultural milieu and finally seek to correlate the two" as a way of reaching beyond their "preunderstandings in order to grasp the biblical message" (1983, 91).

Gration (1984) has presented an extremely practical way of using the questions and issues faced by a specific culture as a stimulus to theologizing. He suggests that contextual theology be done by a group of believers in a specific context who answer four questions: what is the gospel, what is culture, how has the gospel been "good news" for this culture, and where has the gospel not touched or transformed this culture? This last question clarifies the unfinished task of theologizing in any culture by raising issues that need to be addressed from Scripture.[7]

Context, then, can and should form the agenda for theologizing. However, the answers to questions and issues raised by the context must come from exegesis controlled by biblical paradigms. One is not free to roam through Scripture and use any text that seems to casually address the question at hand. Nor is it true that

---

[7] See also Hiebert (1984) for another "issue-centered" approach to doing contextual theology.

> a hermeneutic reading of the biblical message occurs only when the reading *supersedes the first contextual meaning* (not only that of the author but also that of his first readers). This happens *through the unfolding of a surplus-of-meaning disclosed by a new question addressed to the text.* (Croatto 1981, 3)

The purpose of asking questions of the text is not to find answers that are not in the text, but to search for the answers that are already there. Croatto's mistake is the same as that made by many context-based theologians: the cultural context becomes the controlling paradigm which adds to the original meaning of Scripture. Interpreters may find questions for theologizing in the context, but the paradigm established by the text must remain the foundation for seeking the answers which will make up the contextual theology.

When interpreters approach the text seeking to understand the message in its original context, they will often find that their questions are altered by Scripture. Larkin emphasizes that

> through successive exposure to God's Word [interpreters] are able to bring their preunderstanding and, as a result, their interpretation and application closer and closer to alignment with Scripture's truth . . . . At the very heart of the hermeneutical process correctly undertaken is a sanctification process. The Word of God challenges, corrects, and informs the interpreter's preunderstanding, and renews the mind. (Larkin 1988, 302)

Kraft agrees with this concept of a hermeneutical spiral which continually corrects the interpreter's perspective and which will keep theology fresh, relevant, and biblical because it is based on the questions and issues of real life.

> At the beginning of the "spiral" the interpreter goes with certain felt needs to the Scriptures under the guidance of

God and with the assistance of the Christian community
. . . . The interpreter moves from needs to Scripture, to
application in the living of his or her life, to needs
(some of which are newly perceived and at a deeper level),
to Scripture (some of which he or she sees with "new
eyes"), to deeper-level application in the living of his
or her life, etc. . . .

    This dialogical approach to hermeneutics is more
serious than previous approaches in the place it gives to
the interpreter and the receptor group in their respective
contexts. It does not assume either unbiased interpreters
or the universality for all times and places of the
answers arrived at by previous interpreters in their times
and places. It places real people with real needs in
real-life contexts at the center of the hermeneutical
process. (Kraft 1978, 145-146; c.f. Padilla 1980, 76;
<u>Willowbank Report</u> 1978, 10-11).

## Theologizing Incomplete Without Application

One of the most important contributions of liberation theology and its emphasis on context is the reminder that theologizing is incomplete until theology is being practiced in everyday life. Theological understanding and response are closely related for two reasons. First, people always understand in relation to themselves and their own context. "Understanding and meaning operate at the level of practical concern, and not merely theoretical observation" (Thiselton 1980, 31). Second, the Bible itself was written, not only to correct thinking, but to change lives. Texts such as James 1:22-27 and 2 Timothy 3:16-17 clearly demonstrate that the purpose of Scripture is more than mental comprehension, but must include a personal response. If readers do not see a personal connection to their lives, they have not really grasped the meaning of the text. Though a biblical text *speaks* whether it is actualized or performed by anyone, it is not *heard* unless the hearer both understands cognitively and responds actively.[8]

Unfortunately, Western theology has often been perceived as emphasizing "the intellectual and theoretical," and so having "failed to address the real issues which affect how a person lives out what he claims to believe" (Simbo 1983, 31-32). Western, evangelical theology has often seemed remote and irrelevant to people because it has not naturally led to action that touches and changes people's lives. But, as Paulo Friere notes, whenever reflection is present without action, "reflection automatically suffers as well; . . . it becomes an empty word" (Friere 1990, 75). The reflections of preachers and theologians will be empty unless they are building bridges between what the text says and its application to the concerns of ordinary people and unless they themselves are putting their theological reflection into action.

> The gospel must not merely be spoken and repeated; it must also be *communicated*. Similarly in Bible study the student is not only concerned with "facts" and information, but with verdicts on himself. Moreover as he "listens" to the text he will not be content only to use stereotyped sets of questions composed by others, but will engage in a *continuous* dialogue of question and answer, until his own original horizons are creatively enlarged. (Thiselton 1977b, 328)

---

[8] The close connection between understanding and response in the Scriptures and the fact that people always understand in relation to their personal circumstances are two reasons why one should not draw too sharp a distinction between "meaning" and "significance." Meaning and significance should be seen more as two sides of a continuum than as sharply distinct.

Individual readers of Scripture must never stop with trying to understand what the text is saying; they must always look for changes which should be made in their lives. Until they see how the text touches them, they have not adequately understood the text. Preachers and theologians must not only state the facts of what Scripture is saying; they must proclaim the relevance of the text to their generation. Until they enlarge the "original horizons" of their listeners, they have not communicated. The purpose of reflecting on Scripture is ultimately good works, and if the good works and reflection do not flow back and forth, the reflection is itself incomplete.

The context in which theology is done is a reminder that theology "is reflection on God's self-disclosure contained in the Scriptures with the purpose of generating the knowledge of God and better obedience" (Tienou 1983, 98; c.f. Conn 1984, 220). If the reflection is not leading to obedience, the reflection itself is inadequate.

## Context as a Source of Theology?

Context-centered theologians find more than questions and thought patterns in the context. They also find in the context the actual answers to the questions human beings are raising, answers which they claim are part of God's revelation. Some African and Asian theologians find that their cultural patterns and the stories from their ethnic past reveal God. Is there a place for general revelation, including human culture and a specific sociological context, to be a source for theology? Will no theological answers be found outside of the Bible? Are the Scriptures the only source for theology?

Erickson points out that "in theory something can be learned from the study of God's creation" (Erickson 1983, 72). But using human culture and context as a source of theology is filled with dangers, because human culture is itself a mixture of the good, sinful, and neutral (c.f. Larkin 1988, 198-217; Kraft 1978, 103-15). The Bible agrees that God has revealed himself in nature (Psalms 19:1-6; Acts 14:17; Romans 1:19-20), but also makes plain that humankind has rejected and perverted that revelation (Romans 1:18, 21-32). The Bible also emphasizes its own superiority as a revelation of God (e.g. Psalms 19:7-14). Perceptions of God in human culture are cloudy and fuzzy compared to his revelation of himself in the Bible, and only God's special revelation carries the message of salvation.[9]

Cole (1984, 12-13) draws a helpful distinction between absolute and relative data bases for contextualized theology. Though content for theology may be found from both the Scriptures (absolute data base) and the context (relative data base), only the absolute data base carries ultimate authority. Culture may be used as a secondary source of theology, but it

---

[9]One of Kraft's most serious shortcomings is his contention that general revelation is informationally adequate (and only motivationally inadequate) for salvation (Kraft 1979, 216-27; see also Conn's critique of Kraft, 1984, 167-76).

must follow careful exegesis and be secondary to the Scripture in its results.

## Summary

How does context influence the process of theologizing? The translation model understands that all theology is contextual. Interpreters will always read and understand Scripture in the light of their own cultural context. However, by seeking to read the Scripture within the biblical paradigm itself, theologians can adequately understand the essential message of Scripture, and this must be the basis of their theologizing. Because no culture will comprehend all of the implications of any text of Scripture, the universal church can benefit from the insight of the local theologies of every culture. The church in every culture must evaluate itself and the symbols of its culture to determine how the gospel should yet be transforming its society.

## A Comparative Chalcedonian Christology

Though the Christology of Chalcedon was rejected by the Oriental Orthodox churches, it was firmly established in the West as the orthodox statement of faith on the nature of Christ until the nineteenth century. In recent years, Chalcedon has been challenged in the West as inadequate, but the debate has usually assumed the humanity of Jesus and challenged whether or not it is coherent to speak of him as also having a divine nature (e.g., Hick 1977, 1993). To the extent that some Western theologians have argued for the logical coherence of two natures co-existing in one person at the same time (e.g., Davis 1980), the Christological discussions in the West have some relevance for the present discussion.

However, it is beyond the scope of this thesis to interact with these theologians and develop a contemporary Chalcedonian Christology. Erickson (1991) has developed a Christology which adequately answers the most serious objections to Chalcedon and will be used as a contemporary Chalcedonian point of comparison to the Christology of the Ethiopian Orthodox Church.

## The Appropriateness of Erickson's Christology

Erickson is especially appropriate as a representative of contemporary Chalcedonian Christology for two reasons. First, Erickson's understanding of Christ's ontological character is faithful to the meaning and intent of Chalcedon, but does not slavishly adhere to Chalcedonian language. Instead, his fresh statement of the person of Christ responds to current issues in Western Christology. His attempts to both root his theology in Scripture and remain relevant to his times and culture make his Christology a good example of biblically-centered contextual theology. Erickson's conclusions are clearly in the Chalcedonian Christological tradition while recognizing the contextual nature of all theology.

Second, Erickson has interacted with one Western theologian (Leigh 1982) who has argued for a one-nature, non-Chalcedonian statement on the nature of Christ that is strikingly similar to the Ethiopian Orthodox position. Erickson's interaction with Leigh provides an example of how he would respond to the one-nature Christology of the EOC.

Leigh argues that "no person can exist without a nature and no nature can exist apart from some individual that has that nature" (Leigh 1982, 125). It is therefore logically impossible for Christ to have two natures in one person. Instead, he asserts that, like a desk-chair that has all the necessary characteristics of both a desk and a chair, and which therefore is in a unique class by itself, so Jesus Christ is the one-natured God-man who is a unique class by himself.

> Whatever characteristics are essential for a person to be properly called God, Jesus has them. Whatever characteristics are essential for a person to be properly called a man, Jesus has them. That is, even though Jesus has only one nature, he is truly divine and he is truly human. (Leigh 1982, 133)

The essential characteristics of divinity and humanity can be combined, Leigh emphasizes, because man as created in the image of God is not wholly dissimilar to the nature of God. Leigh draws three distinctions between his position and what he calls "historic monophysitism." However, only one of his three distinctions (that historic monophysitism does not require as a prerequisite the doctrine of the *imago Dei*) is true of Ethiopian Orthodox Church's doctrine of the nature of Christ. Leigh's position, therefore, looks very similar to the EOC's formal Christology.

Though attracted to some aspects of Leigh's Christology, Erickson ultimately rejects it because it "raises the question of whether Jesus is coessential with either God or humanity" (Erickson 1991, 538). For example, Leigh questions whether Christ has certain characteristics which would seem to be essential to deity (full omniscience and full omnipotence). Erickson's rejection of Leigh and his adherence to the meaning of Chalcedon while remaining sensitive to contextual issues demonstrates that his Christology is an appropriate twentieth century restatement of the Chalcedonian model against which to compare the EOC's Christology.

## Erickson's Christology

Erickson's two-nature Christology has four preliminary themes. First, far from being entirely unlike his creation, God created the world much like himself. Therefore, "we may look to the nature of nature, so to speak, for clues to the divine nature" (Erickson 1991, 540). Second, though God is perfect and complete and so "cannot develop in the sense of growing toward perfection," neither is he impassible and static. "He is nondevelopmentally dynamic," active in his creation, and feeling its emotions (Erickson 1991, 542). Third, God created human beings in his own image; "divine and human natures are not directly and categorically opposed" (Erickson 1991, 545). Of course, the image of God in human beings has been marred by sin, but fourth, Jesus became a man without sin or a sin nature. "The sin which we find in ourselves, which is so opposed to the nature of God and thus would have been an obstacle to incarnation, was not present in him" (Erickson 1991, 547). Erickson draws these threads together in a preliminary conclusion.

> There is considerable genetic similarity, as it were, between the deity and humanity of Jesus. It is not merely that God united with a part of the creation, or even with a human being. He united with a specific member of the human race who was made in the image of God and free from sin. To judge the possibility of incarnation by appraising empirical human nature (which in turn is being done by fallen human nature) may be as unwise as utilizing information regarding organ transplants between total strangers from different parts of the world to judge the possible success of an organ transplant from one's parent. (Erickson 1991, 548)

Having established that Jesus' divine and human natures are not of two contradictory kinds, but are very similar, Erickson adds two more important considerations to his emerging Christology. First, the incarnation was "kenosis by addition." Jesus did not give up any attributes of deity; rather he added attributes of humanity. Second, there is a distinction between deity and humanity in abstraction and combined in the incarnation. Jesus possessed full deity and humanity, but which

> functioned together in such a way that the manifestation of each now was different from the manifestation of either one alone . . . . Deity which is not united with humanity, possesses all of its attributes actively. (Erickson 1991, 556)

However deity combined with humanity may voluntarily chose to limit the use of some of its divine attributes. "Humanity" in the abstract is what is known about *limited, sinful, fallen* human beings, not of one who is sinless and unfallen--all that God meant for human beings to be. Deity actually combined with perfect humanity will not look entirely like either God or man in the abstract.

Erickson's conclusion is that Jesus has all of the attributes of God and man. However he freely gave up the use of some of those divine attributes so that he would live as a human being. He freely chose to live his life in dependence on and in submission to the Father. His use of his divine attributes while living as a human being was only when the Father allowed it. He had all knowledge, but not in his conscious mind. Knowledge of what he would not have known as a man came only as revealed by the Father. He had all power, but depended on the Father to exercise his supernatural power. He could have been everywhere, but limited himself to the restrictions of a physical body for his time on earth.

Erickson, therefore, rejects a one-nature Christology in favor of a contemporary development of Chalcedon's two nature model. Christ's pre-incarnate divine nature combined with a perfect human nature; the two natures were not so unlike as to prevent the union. The resulting union in one person was unlike either divinity or humanity uncombined with the other. Yet he had all the attributes of perfect humanity and, though not always revealed, all the attributes of deity. While still possessing all divine attributes, he voluntarily gave up the independent use of those attributes. Instead, he depended on the Father to reveal his divinity when it was the Father's will.

Erickson's Christology is a contextual theology: he is primarily interacting with attacks on Chalcedonian Christology from critics in the West. Yet it is also especially appropriate as a representative of a contemporary Chalcedonian Christology against which the non-Chalcedonian theology of the Ethiopian Orthodox Church may be compared. Theological and missiological conclusions about the historical, formal, linguistic and, especially, popular perspectives on the nature of Christ will now be made in light of the contextual nature of theology and Erickson's Chalcedonian Christology.

# CHAPTER 7
## CONCLUSIONS

The questions that prompted this study were primarily theological and missiological. Before these questions can be addressed, however, the research findings themselves should be evaluated and analyzed. The research findings contribute to insight on theological and missiological issues in the Ethiopian context. This reflection on the Ethiopian context, in turn contributes to enhanced understanding of broader issues in contextualized theology.

### Reflections on Research Findings

Christological theologizing in the Alert/Gebre Kristos neighborhood must recognize that most Orthodox believe that Christ came to earth to be the example and savior of mankind and that he was divine and human when he was on earth. However, most Orthodox have a tendency to diminish Christ's humanity; most believe that Christ is no longer human and not an intercessor-mediator (Amharic: *amalaj*). Most believe that Christ had only one nature when he was on earth and that he has only one nature at the present.

When they think of Jesus Christ, most Orthodox in the Alert/Gebre Kristos neighborhood think of his works. They understand that he became a human being to provide salvation. However, many put primary emphasis on his work as an example. Christ showed his followers how to fast, be baptized, teach, and do many good works. They are obliged to follow in his footsteps and do those good works as well. Those speaking to Ethiopian Orthodox about Jesus Christ should recognize that they will understand that, in some sense, he died to save them, but they will probably put greater stress on the things Jesus did which they should also do.

Most Orthodox in the Alert/Gebre Kristos neighborhood agree that Jesus Christ was in some sense both God and man. However with that recognition of his divinity and humanity comes a tendency to diminish Christ's humanity. Though the Ethiopian Orthodox Church officially maintains Christ's complete, perfect humanity, many of those in the church--including many clergy--understand his humanity to be fundamentally different from that of other people. Some believe Apollinarian ideas that the union of his divinity and humanity was so complete that his humanity became a divine humanity. Though the EOC's non-Chalcedonian Christology attempts to maintain Christ's full humanity when he was on earth, popularly many believe his divinity overshadowed his humanity.

Very few subjects feel that Christ acted only as a human being when he said he did not know the time of the Son of Man's return. Most believe that Christ really did know the time of his return, but that he was giving glory to the Father or telling the disciples that this was God's matter and not theirs. The answer of these subjects is in line with official Orthodox teaching that, in his unified divine-human nature, Christ never acted only as a human being. Some subjects, particularly priests, explicitly deny that Christ could ever act as only God or only man.

Most subjects[1] agree that after Christ ascended to heaven he ceased to be human in any sense. After his ascension, Christ returned to the state of being only divine. Some Orthodox in the Alert/Gebre Kristos neighborhood see a close connection between Christ's no longer being human and his not being an intercessor-mediator. Talk about Christ's present state should assume that Orthodox do not believe Christ is presently human or presently an intercessor-mediator.

The idea that Christ could have two natures is strongly rejected by Orthodox living in Alert/Gebre Kristos. Many understand the idea of Christ having two natures as implying that he was double minded, or divided against himself, confirming that Amharic words for "nature" do not imply the same field of meaning as the words used by the Chalcedonian fathers. Others are afraid that speaking of Christ as having a "human nature" will detract from his deity,

---

[1] All women, all but one layman who felt Jesus was God or God-man when on earth, and about half of all clergy felt Jesus was no longer human after his ascension.

confirming the tendency to elevate Christ's deity at the expense of his humanity. Some, particularly clergy, relate one-nature Christology with Christianity which is historically Ethiopian and Orthodox and two-nature Christology with heretical ideas from outside of Ethiopia. If individuals speak of Christ as having "two natures" they are likely to create misunderstanding and give the impression they are not genuinely Ethiopian or orthodox in their Christology.

## Christological Theologizing in Ethiopia

The research findings contribute both to general principals and specific suggestions about Christological theologizing in Ethiopia.

### General Principles

Christological theologizing in Ethiopia must begin with the recognition that all theology is contextual. Statements made about the nature of Christ among Ethiopian Orthodox will be understood in the light of historical, linguistic, formal, and popular perspectives on the nature of Christ held by the Ethiopian Orthodox Church. Evangelicals who seek to do biblically-centered contextual theology will put priority on the biblical paradigm and seek to read Christological passages of Scripture as they were meant to be read. But they must also recognize that their Christological understanding and the way their conclusions are heard will be shaped by the Ethiopian context.

Evangelical theologians in Ethiopia will need to be especially sensitive to issues of form and meaning. One-nature, non-Chalcedonian Christology continues to be a significant symbol (Geertz 1973, 89-93) to many Orthodox. Evangelicals should recognize the importance of this form as they seek to understand the meaning that stands behind biblical explanations of the person and nature of Christ. Evangelicals in the Ethiopian context must carefully probe the meaning behind both Chalcedonian and non-Chalcedonian Christologies and weigh their understandings against the importance of Chalcedonian and non-Chalcedonian forms. They should not feel obligated to use Chalcedonian forms; if they determine that Chalcedonian forms will actually communicate something *other* than biblical meanings in the Ethiopian context, they must find new forms to replace the forms of Chalcedon. At the same time, they should determine the extent to which the non-Chalcedonian forms used by the EOC communicate or contradict biblical meanings. On the one hand, it may be possible to use the Christological forms used by the EOC. On the other hand, it may be necessary to replace EOC Christological forms with forms that will communicate biblical meaning in the clearest, most non-offensive way possible.

Evangelicals in Ethiopia should recognize that both popularly and officially there are differences in Chalcedonian Christology (as represented by Erickson 1991) and the Christology of the EOC. While both accept Christ's deity and humanity, popularly held perspectives on the nature of Christ often question his true, genuine humanity. Some official statements of the EOC also seem to indicate that Christ's deity so influenced his humanity that his humanity was not the same as that of other people. In addition, EOC theologians are unwilling to speak of Christ acting only in his divine or human nature, while Chalcedonian theologians are often willing to say Christ did something in his humanity. Erickson, for example, affirms that Christ lived much of his life without drawing on his divine attributes. He learned and grew as any other human being. He depended on and submitted to the Father for the use of his divine attributes. Though the EOC's formal one-natured Christology agrees with Chalcedonian Christology in its essential affirmations, distinctive differences remain between the two. The question posed by Erickson in answering Leigh remains: can any one-natured Christology maintain *both* Christ's true deity and true humanity.

## Specific Suggestions

Principles for evangelical Christological theologizing in Ethiopia will work themselves out differently depending on the nature of the relationship of evangelicals and the Ethiopian Orthodox which whom they are communicating.

### Initial Contacts of Evangelicals with Ethiopian Orthodox

When evangelicals initially speak with Ethiopian Orthodox about Jesus Christ it is suggested that they simply speak of Christ as being "truly human and truly divine." Use of Amharic words for "nature" should be avoided because the distinct possibility that misunderstanding will be created. Evangelicals do not want to communicate that Christ was divided against himself, that he was two persons, or that they are followers of Nestorius. Evangelicals should stress that they believe that there was only one Christ who was both God and man.

Speaking of Christ as truly divine and truly human is an accurate reflection of Chalcedonian Christology which avoids the potential problems that arise when Amharic words for "nature" are used. Though some Orthodox may object with the use of the word "truly," it reflects language used by the EOC in its own writings. Evangelicals should explain what they mean when they say Christ was truly human: Jesus did and felt everything other people do and feel, with the exception of sin.

Evangelicals should further affirm that they believe that Christ is still human. The basis for their belief should be explained as the perfect union (*tewahedo*) of his deity and humanity. Emphasis on Christ's present humanity will lay the groundwork for explaining why evangelicals do not feel the need for other intercessor-mediators; as a human being, Jesus is himself adequate to serve as intercessor-mediator. However, evangelicals making evangelistic contacts should probably not *initially* stress Christ's position as intercessor-mediator, as it would be misunderstood and create barriers. Initially, it would be sufficient to affirm Christ's present humanity.

Finally, evangelicals should emphasize and carefully explain Christ's work as savior when speaking to Ethiopian Orthodox. Orthodox folk will agree that Christ is certainly savior; evangelical emphasis on Christ as savior will build bridges, clarify areas of potential disagreement, and balance possible Orthodox emphasis on Christ as primarily example.

## In-depth Discussions with Orthodox or Former Orthodox

Evangelicals who establish good relations with Ethiopian Orthodox will have opportunity to further explain their understanding the nature of Christ. In particular, Orthodox who become evangelical Christians will need special instruction to help them have a fuller understanding of evangelical Christology that is genuinely Ethiopian. Evangelical discipleship among the former Orthodox will need to have some particular emphases.

Evangelicals engaging in deeper discussion with Orthodox or former Orthodox should stress the implications of Christ's full humanity when he was on earth and following his ascension. Texts such as Hebrews 2:5-18; 4:14-5:10 and Philippians 2:1-12 should be explored in depth to show that Christ has experienced all human emotion and all human suffering to provide human salvation and so that he can understand and sympathize with all people. Texts such as 1 Timothy 2:5 should be used to demonstrate that Christ remained human after his ascension.

In particular, Christ's present humanity means that he is able to act as intercessor-mediator. Evangelicals should explain that because Jesus is *still* truly God and truly man, he can be both *amalaj* and *temalaj*; he both intercedes and receives intercession. Christ's continuing humanity means that no other intercessor-mediator is necessary; believers have the privilege of going directly to God through the God-man (1 Timothy 2:1-7).

## Evangelical Theological Education

Evangelical theological education programs in Ethiopia must prepare students to do Christological theologizing in the Ethiopian context. Students must recognize the issues surrounding the nature of Christ which will affect their own thinking and the thinking of the people among whom they minister.

First, students in evangelical theological education programs in Ethiopia must themselves become aware of the historical, linguistic, formal, and popular perspectives on the nature of Christ in their own context. Second, they must become aware of the contextual nature of theology. It is not enough for them to either repeat evangelical Christologies from abroad or adopt Ethiopian Orthodox Christology. They must themselves wrestle with the issues and develop a

Christology which reflects their own understanding of Scripture but which also communicates clearly and does not raise unnecessary offense in their own context. All historical and cultural contexts raise particular questions for theologizing, and the Ethiopian context demands that fresh Christological theologizing on the nature of Christ take place.

It is strongly recommended that students in evangelical theological education programs in Ethiopia compare and contrast the strengths of Chalcedonian and non-Chalcedonian Christologies. They should understand that the strength of Chalcedonian Christology is its stress on Christ living a truly human life and that Christ's divinity did not overshadow his humanity. They should understand the strength of non-Chalcedonian Christology is its stress on the union of the one Christ in his person and all his works. Students in evangelical theological education programs in Ethiopia should develop for themselves a Christology for Ethiopia which preserves the best of both and which will not cause misunderstanding or offense.

In December 1996, evangelical students taking a course on theological method at the Evangelical Theological College of Addis Ababa had the opportunity to engage in such fresh Christological theologizing. First, they reviewed the contextual nature of theology. Second, they thoroughly reviewed the contextual factors which shape their theology of the person of Christ. Third, they examined key texts from the Scriptures which provide the content for their understanding of Christ's person. Finally, in small groups of four to six, they wrote a Christological creed for evangelicals in Ethiopia in the last decade of the twentieth century. So that their Christological understanding was truly expressed in the Ethiopian context and so that they would adequately wrestle with the context's unique linguistic issues, the creeds were written in Amharic. However, so that the creeds could explain Ethiopian evangelical Christology to others outside the Ethiopian context and contribute to cross-cultural theology about Christ, they were also translated into English.

The English translations of the creeds written by each of these eight groups are recorded in Appendix B. All eight groups stressed the unity of Christ's divinity and humanity in one personality. Only one of the eight groups chose to say that Christ had "two natures," and this group stressed that by two natures they did "not mean that Christ has two personalities, but that he is one person." Most of the groups chose to speak of the union of Christ's divinity and humanity without using any Amharic word for "nature" at all. Rather, they spoke of Christ being "perfect God and perfect man" and stressed the unmixed, unconfused nature of both his divinity and deity. One group eloquently said that

> being perfect God, he fulfilled everything on earth that created [humans] cannot do. Being perfect man, except for sin, he showed his fleshly nature by becoming tired, trusting, becoming hungry, crying, and especially by

> dying. Christ's deity did not override-abolish[2] or reduce his perfect humanity. Neither did Christ's perfect humanity override-abolish or reduce his deity. We believe these two dwelt together in harmony without conflict, perfectly united in one person.

By stressing Christ's perfect deity and perfect humanity, by emphasizing that his deity and humanity did not abolish or reduce each other, and by stressing the perfect union of his deity and humanity, this group hoped to express a Christology that is clear, biblical, and non-offensive to the Ethiopian context.

Many of the groups incorporated phrases from Orthodox statements on the nature of Christ into their creeds. But the groups did not hesitate to contradict popular Ethiopian Orthodox thinking when they felt those ideas were unbiblical. Several groups stressed that because Christ was perfect man after his ascension, he was the only intercessor-mediator standing between God and human beings.

The exercise in Christological theologizing conducted by these students of the Evangelical Theological College of Addis Ababa demonstrates the importance of Ethiopian evangelicals developing their own Christology. It also demonstrates that such contextual theologies can be both biblical and appropriate to the context.[3]

---

[2] Amharic: *sha-re*.

[3] The Evangelical Churches' Fellowship of Ethiopia has only a brief statement on the person of Christ--which states that he was the Son of God clothed in flesh--as part of a longer statement on Christ as our substitute who provides salvation from sin through his sacrificial death.

## Implications for Biblically-Centered Contextual Theologizing

The findings on perspectives on the nature of Christ in the Ethiopian Orthodox Church have relevance for a broader understanding of the process of theologizing within particular contexts.

### The Contextual Nature of Theology

The entire question of how the nature of Christ should be understood and explained in the Ethiopian context powerfully illustrates the contextual nature of all theology.

On the one hand, Ethiopian Orthodox will hear Chalcedonian statements on the nature of Christ in light of historical and linguistic factors of which Chalcedonian theologians may be totally unaware. Describing Christ as having "two natures" may not imply that he is perfectly human and perfectly divine, but that he is divided against himself. Use of Chalcedonian terminology may imply that the speaker represents foreign or heretical ideas that are not authentically Ethiopian. On the other hand, when Ethiopian Orthodox describe Christ as having "one nature," Chalcedonians may not hear them emphasizing the unity of Christ's person; instead they may understand them to be denying either his true deity or humanity.

Comparison of Ethiopian Orthodox and Chalcedonian Christologies is a reminder that two seemingly contradictory theologies may *both* express certain truths of Scripture and that all theologies are shaped by specific contextual concerns.

## Awareness of Aspects of the Text

Christological perspectives in the EOC clearly illustrate that context influences interpreters' and theologians' awareness of certain aspects of the biblical text. Ethiopian Orthodox are particularly aware of portions of the biblical text that stress the deity of Christ and the complete unity of his person. These texts take on a central place in EOC Christology. Ideas that seem to threaten Christ's full deity or imply any disunity in his person are ruthlessly rejected.

At the same time, perspectives on the nature of Christ in the EOC help Chalcedonian Christians realize that they have stressed biblical texts emphasizing both Christ's deity and humanity and the consequent diversity of his person. Chalcedonian Christians may have underemphasized the unity of Christ's person because of their own unique context.

## Form and Meaning

A comparison of Ethiopian Orthodox and Chalcedonian theologies strongly supports the concept that the relationship between form and meaning must be viewed on a continuum. Both the Chalcedonian ("two natures") and Ethiopian Orthodox ("one nature") verbal forms are used to express the idea that Christ is truly God and truly man. However, in Ethiopia the

Chalcedonian form may also communicate a non-Ethiopian, heretical idea that Christ is divided. But the Ethiopian Orthodox form may lead to Christ being seen as less than genuinely human. The problems created by using either of these forms in the Ethiopian context may demand that a third form (such as "perfect deity and perfect humanity joined in one Christ") would better communicate the truths expressed by Scripture. Theological forms must not be thoughtlessly accepted or discarded. Rather, the implications of using any form in any particular context must be carefully considered before accepting, discarding, or substituting theological forms.

## Inter-cultural Theologizing

A study of EOC perspectives on the nature of Christ is an example of inter-cultural theologizing. Listening carefully to what the EOC has to say about the nature of Christ provides a metacritical check and enrichment for Chalcedonian theologians. The resulting sharing of theologies contributes to a cross-cultural Christology which better reflects the full teachings of Scripture. In particular, the EOC's strong emphasis on the unity of Christ makes an important contribution to the universal church. The EOC rejects Chalcedonian theology because it seems to imply that the deity and humanity of Christ were not perfectly united. Chalcedonian churches must ask themselves if a theology that teaches that Christ did anything--including die--in only one of his natures can ultimately preserve the perfect union of his deity and humanity.

On the other hand, the concerns of Chalcedonian theologians that any Christology must preserve the true humanity of Christ should lead EOC theologians to a closer examination of the implications and possible contradictions within their own theology. EOC theologians should pay special attention to findings which indicate that, despite their formal teachings to the contrary, many of their members do not really accept the genuine humanity of Christ.

## Use of Creeds and Historical Theology

A study of perspectives on the nature of Christ in the EOC also clarifies the use of past creeds and historical theology in the process of theologizing. Among many Western theologians the Chalcedonian creed is considered a fundamental starting point for Christological thinking. The perspectives of the EOC, however, are a reminder that no creed can serve as a clear, unambiguous theological summary for all time. Local contexts may so condition the understanding of a creed that it will never communicate the ideas it was intended to communicate.

Christological theologizing in Ethiopia which seeks to preserve the perfect unity of Christ's true deity and true humanity--the truths Chalcedon sought to express--cannot simply repeat the Chalcedonian creed. However, neither should Chalcedon simply be abandoned. Chalcedon has served the church in many cultures and in many historical periods as concise statement of Scriptural teaching on the nature of Christ. The concerns that lie behind Chalcedon and the creed's particular forms and underlying meanings must all be carefully studied to help ensure that Christological theologizing in Ethiopia remains true to Scripture.

Christological issues in Ethiopia are a reminder that the creeds of the church are useful as a single point of reference for intercultural theology, but they must not become a replacement for fresh theologizing in each historical and cultural context. Each context demands its own reflection on biblical truth and its own statement of the results of that reflection. At the same time, no group that seeks to call itself "Christian" can ignore past creeds. Though they are not the final theological word, creeds--and the context in which *they* were shaped--must be carefully studied to help current theologizing remain reflective of God's universal truth. It is possible, even necessary, for theological statements from two historically different contexts to be different without being disparate.

A study of historical perspectives on the nature of Christ in the EOC is also a reminder of the importance of studying *worldwide* historical theology. Church historians who conclude that Christological debate was settled with Chalcedon and who do not study the ongoing debate in the East and Ethiopia will miss important developments in theology, developments which affect a large number of Christians outside the West and which even influence contemporary Western Christologies (c.f. Leigh 1982 and Erickson 1991). Western theologians who ignore the historical development of Christology outside their own tradition may find their own theology weakened by its limited perspective. A study of worldwide historical theology provides an important metacritical balance to theology developed in any one culture.

Relationship Between Reflection and Action

Examining popular perspectives on the nature of Christ among Ethiopian Orthodox demonstrates how closely theological reflection is related to response and action. A number of subjects drew a connection between Christ not being human in the same way that other people are human (either presently or when he was on earth) and their need for other intercessor-mediators who would better be able to intercede for them. These people have a Christology which, consciously or unconsciously, affects their actions. It would be a serious mistake to assume that these people did not have a Christology or that their Christological beliefs had no effect on their actions. It would be equally serious to teach Christology in this context without applying Christ's nature as perfectly human to his accessibility as sympathetic intercessor-mediator. The contextual nature of theology clearly demonstrates that theologizing is incomplete without personal application.

## Suggestions for Missionary Training

A study of perspectives on the nature of Christ in the Ethiopian Orthodox Church also suggests some guidelines for training cross-cultural missionaries. Most cross-cultural missionaries are aware that they will need to study the culture of their new country and make cultural adjustments. Most also realize that they will need to study the religious views of the people with whom they are working. However, many do not realize the importance of studying the theological history of their new country or of comparing official religious teaching with popular religious understanding.

Present official and popular perspectives on the nature of Christ among Ethiopian Orthodox can not be understood by outsiders unless they study the history of the ancient church or the history of Christological development in Ethiopia. The theology of Cyril and a hatred of Nestorius are alive among Orthodox clergy; anyone seeking to talk with these clergy about Christ will need to understand ancient church history. Understanding the sixteenth and seventeenth century clashes between the Orthodox and the Jesuits makes intelligible many of the Orthodox's present theological concerns. And even though Orthodox debates over the anointing of Christ seem distant and irrelevant to many Westerners, missionaries who do not understand the issues may find themselves creating needless offense among Orthodox. Well-prepared cross-cultural missionaries will study the historical development of theology and religion in their new cultures.

Cross-cultural missionaries should also probe the relation between formal "high" religion and popular "low" religion in their new cultures. The Ethiopian Orthodox Church officially maintains the full deity and full humanity of Jesus Christ. However, many Orthodox in the Alert/Gebre Kristos neighborhood find it difficult to affirm the genuine humanity of Christ. Missionaries must be aware that what they learn from books about the formal religion of their new countries may not be what people popularly believe or practice.

Missionary work of all kinds must begin with listening to and learning from people themselves. A valuable tool in understanding popular religion is training in ethnographic research. Cross-cultural missionaries should have some training in ethnographic observation and listening to enhance their ability to learn about popular religion.

## Suggestions for Further Study

An ethnographic study of one neighborhood in Addis Ababa is not an adequate base for drawing general conclusions on popular perspectives on the nature of Christ in the Ethiopian Orthodox Church. An important next step should be synthesizing the findings of this study in a survey that could measure how broadly the perspectives represented in the Alert/Gebre Kristos neighborhood are held throughout Addis Ababa and Ethiopia. The survey would give opportunity for a quantitative testing of the theories suggested by these qualitative findings.

The findings of this study also suggest the need for further qualitative studies. For example, to what extent does the history of the development of Christology in Ethiopia affect present perspectives on the nature of Christ among the clergy? Do clergy throughout the country remember the Jesuits? Do clergy throughout the country relate present evangelicals with the Jesuits and with Suseneyos? What is the exact nuance of the words *baheriy* and *tebay* among laity? How widely are those nuances held? Questions such as these can only be answered by further qualitative ethnographic studies.

Finally, throughout the process of interviewing people in the Alert/Gebre Kristos neighborhood, the relationship of Christology and Soteriology repeatedly surfaced. Further ethnographic questioning needs to be done to explore how Christ's past and present nature as God, man, and intercessor-mediator relate to the way in which he functions as savior. If Christ is perceived as truly man after his ascension, will he be more readily accepted as an *amalaj*? To what degree is Christ's intercessor-mediatorship and his perceived distance related to the way people seek to appropriate his work as savior? It seems probable that a close relationship exists between popular Christology and popular Soteriology, and the nature of that relationship needs to be explored.

## Conclusion

Theologizing is a process that never ends. The best theologies and creeds can never be the final word on any subject because they represent theological reflection in only one historical, cultural context. Fresh theologizing is the privilege and obligation of God's people in every culture and period of history. Such theologizing must include a careful study of the context in which reflection on and proclamation of God's revelation will take place. A study of perspectives on the nature of Christ in the Ethiopian Orthodox Church has demonstrated the importance of a thorough understanding of the Ethiopian context before Christology is developed or taught in Ethiopia. It has also illustrated that theologizing demands a thorough knowledge of the ever-changing human contexts in which God's eternal revelation is understood and applied. All theologians must thoroughly explore their context as a part of the on-going task of theologizing.

# APPENDIX A

## EOC POSITIONS ON CHRIST'S ANOINTING

| Time | Positions | | |
|---|---|---|---|
| early 1600s – mid 1700s | **Name:** Tewahedo (Union)<br>**Clerical Support:** Monastic order of Tekle Haimenot.<br>**Location:** Shewa<br>**Belief:** The anointing gave Christ a perfect human nature. "The Son the anointer, the anointed, and the anointing." | **Name:** Qebat (Unction)<br>**Clerical Support:** Monastic order of Ewostatiows.<br>**Location:** Gojjam<br>**Belief:** The anointing caused the union of Christ's human and divine natures. "The Father the anointer, the Son the anointed, and the Spirit the anointing." | |

(Most of the Tekle Haimanot clergy and the area of Shewa adopted the new Sost Ledet position; the old Tewahedo position was given the name "Kara" and was maintained by a minority of clergy and in Tigre.)

| Time | Positions | | |
|---|---|---|---|
| mid-1700s – 1878 | **Name:** Sost Ledet/ Yetsegga Leg<br>**Location:** Shewa, Gondor<br>**Beliefs:** Christ was born 3 times: eternally of the Father, temporally of the Virgin Mary, as "Son of Grace." | **Name:** Karra<br>**Location:** Tigre<br>**Beliefs:** same as Tewahedo above. | **Name:** Qebat<br>**Location:** Gojjam<br>**Beliefs:** same as Qebat above. |
| After 1878 | **Name:** Sost Ledet/ Yetsegga Leg<br>**Status:** a sect popular in Gondor. | **Name:** Tewahedo<br>**Status:** Official position nationwide. | **Name:** Qebat<br>**Status:** a sect popular in Gojjam. |

# APPENDIX B

## CHRISTOLOGICAL CREEDS WRITTEN BY STUDENTS OF THE EVANGELICAL THEOLOGICAL COLLEGE OF ADDIS ABABA

<u>Group One</u>: Mezmur W/Mariam, Dansa Dana, Mulugeta Ashagre, Tassew Chefo

We believe that Jesus Christ is perfect man and perfect God. The two natures of Christ were manifested without change, without division in Christ Jesus. By this we do not mean that Christ has two personalities, but that he is one person.

<u>Group Two</u>: Seble Belachew, Akililu Lalego, Ermias Mamo, Michael Zewdie, Zerihun Hailu

Christ had two natures--a divine nature and a human nature--in one person. The two natures do not mean two wills or two thoughts, but his human nature and divine nature--without separating or combining--were revealed in one personality. Because he is the only God-man he can intercede (1 Timothy 2:5, Hebrews 7:25). We believe that both before and after his resurrection Jesus Christ remained in the two natures.

<u>Group Three</u>: Nega Haile, Desalegn Abebe, Tesfaye Robele, Worku Haile Mariam

We believe Jesus Christ is perfect God, the creator and mover of all things, who was equal with God, the eternal Word, greater than the angels, prophets, and priests. We believe that being God, and without reducing his divinity, and being man, without reducing his humanity, but holding onto both, he was conceived of the Holy Spirit and born of the virgin Mary. We believe that by obeying God and emptying himself he became the only one standing between God and man as an intercessor-mediator. We believe he is God in one person and one being.

<u>Group Four</u>: Solomon Tilahun, Zerefa Wudneh, Alem Kedane, Seblewengel Daniel, Samuel Beyene

I. The Nature or Being of Christ

A. His deity - We believe in the Son who is equal in existence with the Father and the Holy Spirit, and who is not created but eternal.

B. His humanity - We believe in the Son, who is God and who has revealed himself in the flesh through the virgin birth from Mary. Because he has human flesh, he is fully human and because he is the one and only Son of God he is fully God, but he is one person, Jesus Christ.

II. The Work of Christ

We believe that the Son has paid the price for our sins by his death on the cross and his resurrection from the grave and that he is our mediator.

III. The Second Coming of Christ

We believe that Christ is enthroned in glory at the right side of the Almighty God and that he will comes in glory as the final judge who will punish sinners eternally and reward the righteous eternally.

Group Five: Yuseph Menna, Yohannes Girma, Behailu Shibru, Mihratu Petros

Jesus has one personality. We believe that his deity and humanity joined in the one personality, without any confusion, without any change, without any division.

Group Six: Minus Bruk, Bulutse Futuwi, Henock Asfaw, Samuel Seifu

We believe that Christ, being eternal God and the second person of the Trinity, was conceived in time by saint Virgin Mary of the power of the Holy Spirit, and was born but not created. Christ is perfect God and perfect man. Being perfect God, he fulfilled everything on earth that created [humans] cannot do. Being perfect man, except for sin, he showed his fleshly nature by becoming tired, trusting, becoming hungry, crying, and especially by dying. Christ's deity did not override-abolish (*shar-e*) or reduce his perfect humanity. Neither did Christ's perfect humanity override-abolish or reduce his deity. We believe these two dwelt together in harmony without conflict, perfectly united in one person. We believe that Jesus Christ came to earth to save men and, after accomplishing redemption, he arose in heavenly glory and lives forever in divine glory in his perfect humanity and perfect deity.

<u>Group Seven</u>: Henock Tadesse, Alemayhu Goshu, Menase Desalegn, Shewangezaw Lulie

Jesus Christ is perfect God and perfect man. He is one, with one nature, one character. The nature of God the Father and God the Son are one. The character of God the Father and God the son are one. The difference is in their person.

<u>Group Eight</u>: Tesfaye Sime, Yared Alemayehu, Gebru Argaw, Wondimu Abebe, Deborah Tegegnework

Jesus Christ is fully God and fully man. He is the Son of God and so he has the nature of God. He was conceived by the Holy Spirit and born of the virgin Mary. Jesus Christ is fully God and fully man, without mixture of his divinity and humanity, in one person.

# GLOSSARY OF AMHARIC TERMS

Akal (አካል). The most common word to describe the "person" of Christ or the "persons" of the Godhead.

Amalaj (አማላጅ; plural: amalajoch; አማላጆች). Angels or saints who stand between God and human beings, who intercede or mediate to God for human beings, and who are consequently the recipients of prayer and honor by most members of the Ethiopian Orthodox Church.

Baheriy (ባሕሪይ). The most frequently used Amharic or Ge'ez word used for the "nature" of Christ, meaning "nature, character, essence, personality, trait, attribute, temperament" (Laslau 1976, 85).

Debtara (ደብተራ). The cantor-teachers of the Ethiopian Orthodox Church who gain their status through their knowledge of holy books and traditions, giving them spiritaual and magical power.

Helawi (ሕላዌ). "Being, existence," sometimes used theologically to refer to the "nature" of Christ (Laslau 1976, 1).

Karra (ካራ). The derogatory nickname of "knife" given to the Tewahedo position of the Ethiopian Orthodox Church because it "cut off" the third birth of Christ (see *Sost Ledet*).

Meri-gaeta (መሪ ጌታ). A title indicating a high level of formal theological education, such as a "doctor of theology."

Qebat (ቅባት). The "anointing" or "unction" sect of the Ethiopian Orthodox Church, which believes that Christ's anointing affected the union of his natures and that the Father is the anointer, the son, the anointed, the Holy Spirit the anointing oil.

Sost Ledet (or Yesost Ledet; የሶስት ልደት). The "three births" sect of the Ethiopian Orthodox Church, which believes that Christ was born three times--eternally of the Father, temporally of the virgin Mary, and to be "Son of

God by Grace" (see *Yetsegga Leg*), either in Mary's womb or when he was baptized in the River Jordan.

Tabot (ታቦት). The flat, rectangular wooden box, or "ark," which serves as a representation of the Ark of the Covenant and which consecrates an Ethiopian Orthodox church builing. Each *tabot* has the name of one of the saints of the EOC (all of whom can serve as *almejoch*) and the *tabot* gives its name to its church. Many members of the Ethiopian Orthodox Church will commonly equate the *tabot* itself with the saint for whom it is named.

Tebay (ጠባይ). "Nature, character, disposition, conduct, temperament," often used to refer to the "nature' of Christ (Laslau 1976, 231); also pronounced "tsebay".

Temalaj (ተማላጅ). Passive form of "*amalaj*," one who receives intercession or mediation; usually reserved for God himself.

Tewahedo (ተዋሕዶ). The official "union" teaching of the Ethiopian Orthodox Church that Christ was anointed before birth when his two natures fused into one nature--the anointing restoring to Christ's humanity what was lost in Adam's fall--and that the Son himself was the anointer, the anointed and the ointment of anointing.

Yetsegga Leg (የጸጋ ልጅ). An incipient form of the *Sost Ledet* sect which taught "that Christ was not co-eternal with the Father but was adopted Son of God by grace at his baptism" (Aren 1978, 77).

# REFERENCE LIST

Alemayehu Moges. 1995a (1987 Ethiopian Calendar). *Hulum hulun yeweq*. [Let everyone know everything]. Addis Ababa: N.p.

_____. 1995b. Interview by author, 25 July, Addis Ababa.

Alemu Mansebo. 1996. Interview by author, 13 July, Addis Ababa Werede 23, Kebelle 16 office, Addis Ababa.

Aren, Gustav. 1978. *Evangelical pioneers in Ethiopia: Origins of the evangelical church Mekane Yesus*. Stockholm: EFS Forlaget.

Asarat Gebre Maryam. 1991 (1983 E.C.). *Temhert melekot*. [Spiritual education]. Addis Ababa: Artistic Printers.

Ayala Takla Haymanot. 1981. *The Ethiopian church and its Christological doctrine*. Addis Ababa: Graphic Printers.

Aymro Wondmagegnehu and Joachim Motovu. 1970. *The Ethiopian Orthodox Church*. Addis Ababa: The Ethiopian Orthodox Mission.

Bahru Zewde. 1991. *A history of modern Ethiopia: 1855-1974*. Addis Ababa: Addis Ababa University Press.

Bailey, Kenneth E. 1976. *Poet and peasant*. Grand Rapids, Mich.: Eerdmans.

_____. 1980. *Through peasant eyes*. Grand Rapids, Mich.: Eerdmans.

Barzun, Jacques, and Henry F. Graff. 1992. *The modern researcher*. 5th edition. Fort Worth: Harcourt Brace Jovanovich.

Bekele Mekuria. 1995. Interview by author, 12 June, Addis Ababa. Wereda 24, Kebelle 15 office, Addis Ababa.

Berhanu Gobena. 1993 (1985 E.C.). *Amde haimanot*. [Pillar of faith]. Addis Ababa: By the author

Bevans, Stephen. 1985. Models of contextual theology. *Missiology* 13, no. 13 (April): 185-202.

Blyth, E. M. E. 1935. The church of Ethiopia. *The Hibbert Journal* 34: 80-91.

Bogden, Robert C., and Sari Knopp Bilken. 1982. *Qualitative research for education*. Boston: Allyn and Bacon.

Bonk, Jonathan James. 1972. An annotated and classified bibliography of English literature pertaining to the Ethiopian Orthodox church: A guide for missions. M.A. thesis, Trinity Evangelical Divinty School.

Brake, Donald L. 1977. A historical investigation of monophysitism in the Ethiopian Orthodox church. Th.D. diss., Dallas Theological Seminary.

Budge, E. A. Wallis. 1928. *A history of Ethiopia*. 2 vols. London: Methuen & Co. Ltd.

Carr, Edward H. 1961. *What is history?* New York: Vintage Books.

Chang, Peter. 1981. Steak, potato, peas and chopsuey: Linear and non-linear thinking in theological education. *Evangelical Review of Theology* 5, no. 2 (October): 279-86.

Cole, Victor. 1984. How can we Africanize our faith: Another look at the contextualization of theology. *East Africa Journal of Evangelical Theology* 3, no. 2: 3-20.

Conn, Harvie M. 1978. Contextualization: A new dimension for cross-cultural hermeneutic. *Evangelical Missions Quarterly* 14, no. 1 (January): 39-48.

_____. 1984. *Eternal word and changing world*. Phillipsburg, N.J.: Presbyterian and Reformed Publishing.

Croatto, J. Severino. 1981. *Exodus: A hermeneutics of freedom*. Maryknoll, N.Y.: Orbis.

Crummey, Donald. 1972. *Priests and politicians: Protestant and catholic missions in orthodox Ethiopia 1830-1868*. Oxford: At the Clarendon Press.

Davis, Stephen T. 1980. Is "truly God and truly man" coherent? *Christian Scholars Review* 9, no. 3: 215-224.

Dickson, Kwesi. 1984. *Theology in Africa*. Maryknoll, N.Y.: Orbis.

Eadie, Douglas G. 1973. Chalcedon revisited. *Journal of Ecumenical Studies* 10, no. 1 (Winter): 140-45.

Erickson, Millard. 1983. *Christian theology*. Grand Rapids, Mich.: Baker.

_____. 1991. *The Word became flesh*. Grand Rapids, Mich.: Baker.

_____. 1993. *Evangelical interpretation*. Grand Rapids, Mich.: Baker.

Ephraim Isaac. 1971. Social structure of the Ethiopian church. *Ethiopian Observer* 14, no. 3: 240-288.

Ethiopian Orthodox Tewahedo Church Holy Synod (EOTCHS). 1983. *YeIteyopeya ortodoks tewahedo beite krestiyan acher yetarik yehaymanotena yeserat metsehaf*. [A short history, faith, and order of the Ethiopian orthodox tewahedo church]. Addis Ababa: Tensae Zegoubae Press.

Ethnograph, The. Version 3.0. Qualis Research Associates, Amherst, Mass.

Fetterman, David M. 1989. *Ethnography, step by step*. Applied Social Research Methods Series, vol. 17. Newbury Park, London, New Delhi: Sage Publications.

Fischer, David Hackett. 1970. *Historians' fallacies: Toward a logic of historical thought*. New York: Harper & Row.

Freire, Paulo. 1990. *The pedagogy of the oppressed*. New York: Continuum.

Frend, W. H. C. 1972. *The rise of the monophysite movement: Chapters in the history of the church in the fifth and sixth centuries*. Cambridge: University Press.

Geddes, Michael. 1696. *The Church-history of Ethiopia*. London: Hi Chiswell.

Geertz, Clifford. 1968. *Islam observed: Religious development in Morocco and Indonesia*. New Haven: Yale University Press.

_____. 1973. *The interpretation of cultures*. n.p.: Basic Books.

_____. 1983. *Local knowledge*. n.p: Basic Books.

_____. 1988. *Works and lives: The anthropologist as author*. Stanford, Calif.: Standford University Press.

Gilliland, Dean S. 1989. Contextual theology as incarnational mission. In *The Word among us: Contextualizing theology for mission today*, ed. Dean S. Gilliland, 9-31. Dallas: Word.

Gration, John. 1984. Willowbank to Zaire: The doing of theology. *Missiology*. 12, no. 3 (July): 297-309.

Grillmeier, Aloys, S. J. 1995. *Christ in christian tradition*. Translated by John Cawte and Pauline Allen. Louisville, Ky.: Westminster John Knox.

Habte Mariam Worquineh. 1964-1965. The mystery of the incarnation. *The Greek Orthodox Theological Review* 10, no. 2 (Winter): 154-61.

_____. Nd. *YeIteyopeya ortodoks tewahedo bete krestiyan emenetena temhert*. [The faith and teaching of the Ethiopian orthodox tewahedo church]. Addis Ababa: Berhanina Selam Printing Press.

Hesselgrave, David J., and Edward Rommen. 1989. *Contextualization: Meanings, methods, and models*. Grand Rapids, Mich.: Baker.

Hick, John, ed. 1977. *The myth of God incarnate*. London: SCM Press.

_____. 1993. *The methaphor of God incarnate: Christology in a pluralistic age*. Louisville, Ky.: Westminster John Knox.

Hiebert, Paul G. 1984. Critical contextualization. *Missiology* 12, no. 3 (July): 287-96.

_____. 1989. Form and meaning in the contextualization of the gospel. In *The Word among us: Contextualizing theology for mission today*, ed. Dean S. Gilliland, 101-20. Dallas: Word.

Hirsch, E. D., Jr. 1967. *Validity in interpretation*. New Haven and London: Yale University Press.

Hundley, Raymond. 1993. Towards an evangelical theology of contextualization. Ph.D. diss., Trinity Evangelical Divinity School.

Hyatt, Harry Middleton. 1928. *The church of Abyssinia*. London: Luzac & Co.

Imbakom Kalewold. 1970. *Traditional Ethiopian church education*. Translated by Menghestu Lemma. New York: Teachers College Press, Columbia University.

Johnstone, Patrick. 1993. *Operation World*. Grand Rapids, Mich.: Zondervan.

Jowett, William. 1824. *Christian researches in the Mediterranean from 1815-1820 in furtherance of the objects of the church missionary society*. London: L. B. Seely and Son and J. Hatchard and Son.

Jones, A. H. M., and Elizabeth Monroe. 1935. *A history of Ethiopia*. Oxford: At the Clarendon Press.

Kaplan, Steven. 1984. *The monastic holy man and the christianization of early Solomonic Ethiopia*. Wiesbaden: Steiner.

Kidan Wolde Kifle. N.d. *Metsehafe sewasew weges wemezegebe oalat hadis*. [New Grammar and Dictionary]. N.p.

Kraft, Charles. 1979. *Christianity in culture*. Maryknoll, N.Y.: Orbis.

Larkin, William J., Jr. 1988. *Culture and biblical hermeneutics*. Grand Rapids, Mich.: Baker.

Leigh, Ronald. 1982. Jesus: The one-natured God-man. *Christian Scholars Review* 11, no. 2: 124-137.

Leslau, Wolf. 1976. *Concise Amharic dictionary*. Wiesbaden: Otto Harrassowitz.

Levine, Donald. 1964. On the history and culture of the Manz. *Journal of Semitic Studies* 9, no. 1 (Spring): 204-11.

_____. 1965. *Wax and gold: Tradition and innovation in Ethiopian culture*. Chicago: University of Chicago Press.

_____. 1974. *Greater Ethiopia*. Chicago: University of Chicago Press.

Lichtman, Allan J., and Valerie French. 1978. *Historians and the living past: The theory and practice of historical study*. Arlington Heights, Ill.: Harlan Davidson.

Lindbeck, George A. 1984. *The nature of doctrine: Religion and theology in a postliberal age*. Philadelphia: Westminster.

Lipsky, George Arthur. 1962. *Ethiopia: Its people, its society, its cultures*. New Haven: HRAF Press.

Ludolphus, Job. 1682. *A new history of Ethiopia*. Translated by J. P. Gent. London: Samuel Smith.

Marshall, Catherine and Gretchen B. Rossman. 1989. *Designing qualitative research*. Newbury Park, Calif.: Sage Publications.

Matthew, A. F., ed. 1936. *The teaching of the Abyssinian church as set forth by the doctors of the same*. London: The Faith Press, Ltd.

Mekarios, Abraham, Nathanael, and Batholomews, eds. 1996. *The Ethiopian orthodox tewahedo church faith, order of worship and ecumenical relations*. Addis Ababa: Tensae Publishing House.

Messing, Simon David. 1957. The highland-plateau Amhara of Ethiopia. Ph.D. diss., University of Pennsylvania.

Monette, Duane R., Thomas J. Sullivan and Cornell R. DeJong. 1990. *Applied social research: Tool for the human services*. Fort Worth: Holt, Rinehart and Winston.

*Monitor* (Addis Ababa). 1995. Begging to learn or learning to beg--child theologians in Addis on a "scholarship". 20 June, 3.

Muller, Richard A. 1991. The role of church history in the study of systematic theology. In *Doing theology in today's world: Essay's in honor of Kenneth S. Kantzer*, ed. John D. Woodbridge and Thomas Edward McComiskey, 77-98. Grand Rapids, Mich.: Zondervan.

Musay Tesfa Giorgis. 1997. Interview by author, 8 January, Addis Ababa. Holy Savior Catholic Church, Addis Ababa.

Muzorewa, Gwinyai H. 1985. *The origins and development of African theology*. Maryknoll, N.Y.: Orbis.

Osborne, Grant. 1991. *The hermeneutical spiral: A comprehensive introduction to biblical interpretation*. Downers Grove, Ill.: InterVarsity.

Padilla, Rene. 1980. Hermeneutics and culture: A theological perspective. In *Down to earth: studies in Christianity and culture*. ed. John R. W. Stott and Robert Coote, 63-78. Grand Rapids, Mich.: Eerdmans.

_____. 1983. Biblical foundations: a Latin American study. *Evangelical Review of Theology* 7, no. 1 (April): 79-88.

Papandreou, Damaskinos, and Bishoy of Damiette. 1990. Joint commission of the theological dialogue between the orthodox church and the oriental orthodox churches. Geneva: Orthodox Centre of the Ecumenical Patriarchate. Photocopied.

_____. 1993. Joint commission of the theological dialogue between the orthodox church and the oriental orthodox churches: Communique. Geneva: Orthodox Centre of the Ecumenical Patriarchate. Photocopied.

Pelikan, Jaroslav. 1971. The emergence of the catholic tradition (100-600). Vol. 1, The Christian tradition: A history of the development of doctrine. Chicago: University of Chicago Press.

Poladian, Bishop Terenig. 1964. The doctrinal position of the monophysite churches. Ethiopian Observer 7 (Fall): 257-64.

Reminick, Ronald Allen. 1973. The Manze Amhara of Ethiopia: A study of authority, masculinity, and sociality. Ph.D. diss., University of Chicago.

Richardson, Don. 1984. Eternity in their hearts. Ventura, Calif.: Regal Books.

Sawyer, Harry. 1968. Creative evangelism: Towards a new Christian encounter with Africa. London: Lutterworth Press.

Schaff, Philip. 1877. The creeds of christendom with a history and critical notes. Vol. 2, The Greek and Latin creeds with translations. Grand Rapids, Mich.: Baker.

Schreiter, Robert J. 1985. Constructing local theologies. Maryknoll, N.Y.: Orbis.

Seeyoum Gebre Sellassie. 1995. Interview by author, 3 March, Addis Ababa. Department of Sociology, Addis Ababa University, Addis Ababa.

Sergew Hable Sellassie. 1972. Ancient and medieval Ethiopian history to 1270. Addis Ababa: United Printers.

Shenk, Calvin. 1988. The Ethiopian orthodox church: A study in indigenization. Missiology 16, no. 3 (July): 259-78.

Simbo, Billy K. 1983. An African critique of western theology. Evangelical Review of Theology 7, no. 1 (April): 28-33.

Spradley, James P. 1979. The ethnographic interview. New York: Holt, Rinehart, Winston.

Stackhouse, Max L. 1988. Contextualization, contextuality, and contextualism. In One faith, many cultures, ed. Ruy O. Costa, 3-13. Boston Theological Institute Annual Series, vol. 2. Maryknoll, N.Y.: Orbis.

Strauss, Steve. 1980. The application of the gospel of Luke. Th.M. thesis, Dallas Theological Seminary.

_____. 1990. Review of Culture and biblical hermeneutics, by William Larkin. In Africa Journal of Evangelical Theology 9, no. 1: 59-64.

Sundkler, Bengt. 1979. Towards a Christian theology in Africa. In Readings in dynamic indigeneity, ed. Charles H. Kraft and Tom N. Wisley, 493-515. Pasadena, Calif.: William Carey Library.

Taber, Charles R. 1978. Is there more than one way to do theology? Gospel in context 1, no. 1 (January): 4-10.

Taddesse Tamrat. 1970. Persecution and religious controversies. In The church of Ethiopia: A panorama of history and spiritual life, ed. Sergew Hable Sellassie, 27-30. Addis Ababa: Haile Selassie I University Press.

_____. 1972. Church and state in Ethiopia: 1270-1527. Oxford: Clarendon Press.

Tesfazghi Uqbit. 1973. Current Christological positions of Ethiopian orthodox theologians. Rome: Pontificia Institutum Studiorum Orientalium.

Teshager Wube. 1959. The wandering student. University College of Addis Ababa Ethnological Society Bulletin 9 (July-December): 52-60.

Third and fourth consultations between eastern orthodox and oriental orthodox theologians: The Geneva and the Addis Ababa consultations. 1971. The Greek Orthodox Theological Review 16, nos. 1 and 2 (Spring and Fall): 3-235.

Thistleton, Anthony C. 1977a. Semantics and new testament interpretation. In New testament interpretation: Essays on principles and methods, ed. I. Howard Marshall, 75-104. Grand Rapids, Mich.: Eerdmans.

_____. 1977b. The new hermeneutic. In New testament interpretation: Essays on principles and methods, ed. I. Howard Marshall, 308-33. Grand Rapids, Mich.: Eerdmans.

_____. 1980. *The two horizons: New testament hermeneutics and philosophical description*. Grand Rapids, Mich.: Eerdmans.

_____. 1992. *New horizons in hermeneutics*. Grand Rapids, Mich.: Zondervan.

Thiselton, Anthony C., Roger Lundin, and Clarence Walhout. 1985. *The responsibility of hermeneutics*. Grand Rapids, Mich.: Eerdmans.

Tienou, Tite. 1983. Biblical foundations: An African study. *Evangelical Review of Theology* 7, no. 1 (April): 89-101.

_____. 1984. The church in African theology: Description and analysis of hermeneutical presuppositions. In *Biblical interpretation and the church: Text and context*, ed. D. A. Carson, 151-65. Grand Rapids, Mich.: Baker.

*The Willowbank report: Gospel and culture*. 1978. By John Stott, Chairman. Charlotte, N.C.: Lausanne Committee for World Evangelization.

Yeshaq. 1989. *The Ethiopian tewahedo church: An integrally African church*. New York: Vantage Press.